SURVIVING

THE DEATH OF

A SIBLING

SURVIVING THE DEATH OF A SIBLING

Living Through Grief When an Adult Brother or Sister Dies

T. J. WRAY

Foreword by Dr. Earl Thompson

THREE RIVERS PRESS • NEW YORK

Published by Three Rivers Press, New York, New York.
Member of the Crown Publishing Group, a division of Random House, Inc.
www.randomhouse.com

THREE RIVERS PRESS and the Tugboat design are
registered trademarks of Random House, Inc.

Printed in the United States of America

DESIGN BY BARBARA STURMAN

Library of Congress Cataloging-in-Publication Data
Wray, T. J.
    Surviving the death of a sibling: living through grief when an adult
brother or sister dies / T. J. Wray.
Includes bibliographical references.
    1. Consolation. 2. Death—Religious aspects—Christianity.
3. Bereavement—Religious aspects—Christianity. 4. Grief—Religious
aspects—Christianity. 5. Wray, T. J. I. Title.
    BV4905.3 .W73 2003
    155.9'37'0855—dc21   2002154212

ISBN 0-609-80980-6

10 9

First Edition

For you, Mom, with love and gratitude

And in memory of my brother,
whose gentle, guiding spirit is present in these words

Acknowledgments

I'm deeply grateful to my husband, Rob, for his love, emotional support, and editorial assistance. Thank you for always taking the time to affirm the importance of this work. I'm equally indebted to my children, Bob, Anne, and Jack, whose encouragement and hugs have sustained me throughout this process. Thank you for saying "We're proud of you, Mom" on those days when I needed to hear it most. Whatever else I may do in this world, it will pale in comparison to having had the honor of being your mother.

I'm also grateful to my parents, Valerie and Curt, and to my sisters, Linda, Robin, and Tracy, for their love and support, especially during that first terrible year without our beloved VJay.

I'd like to thank Walter Burr for believing in this project from the beginning and for helping me to take those first difficult steps necessary to make this book a reality. I'm also grateful to Anne McFadden, Nancy Rosenberg, Donna Bowen, Louise Doire, Regina Ballard, Jill Newman, Janet Alexander, Nancy Rockefeller, Elaine Macmillan, Jayme Hennessy, Judy Bailey, Claire Stanley, and all the other strong and beautiful women who have graced my life with love and friendship.

Thanks to my many wonderful students, friends, and colleagues at Salve Regina University. In particular, I'd like to recognize the members of the Religious Studies Department for their affirmation and support. I'm honored to be part of such a fine group of scholars and compassionate individuals. Thanks, also, to Earl Thompson and everyone at Andover Newton Theological School for their caring support and prayerful presence.

A special note of appreciation to my agent extraordinaire, Rob McQuilkin, who helped me to find my "writer's voice" and to my wonderfully talented editor, Orly Trieber, whose sensitivity to the material, invaluable suggestions, and friendship have been a special blessing. Thanks, also, to editorial director Becky Cabaza for her flexibility and understanding and to Betsy Rapoport for her early support of this project.

Many thanks to Laureen and Shell for their dedication to preserving the community spirit of the adult sibling grief website (www.adultsiblinggrief.com), and to my webmaster, Dave Castiglioni, for his creativity and friendship.

Finally, I'm profoundly grateful to the thousands of surviving siblings who have shared their journeys of loss with me. In particular, I'd like to recognize all those who contributed to this book—both surviving siblings and their beloved brothers and sisters whose loss is deeply mourned. Their stories have helped me to better understand and articulate this particular type of grief and for that, I'm most humbly grateful to:

Andrea and Ed; Ann and Forest; Betty and Bill; B. G. and Allen; Brad and Bryan; Carl and Greg; Carol and Kathleen; Carolyn and Dougie, Denny; Clare and Andrew; Darcey and Donna; Dean and Stefani; Debra and Lori; Dorothy and Warren; Elise and Judith; Francesca and Larry; Frank and Marshall; Harri and Gail; Heidi and Michael; Helen and JoAnn; Jan and Eddie, Dennis, Dwayne; Janet and Jim; J. Elizabeth and Nancy; Jerry and Barbara; Jill and Debra; Judith and Suzanne; Julianne and Scott; Julie and Bill; Kathleen and Nora, Ricky; Kathryn and Scott; Kathy-Anne and Patsy; Kathy B. and Tommy; K. M. G. and Peter; L. B. and Paul; Linda and Pat; Linda-Lee and Danny; Lisa and Robert; Lisa-Marie and Andy; Marie and Doug, Tom; Martha and Paula, Michael, Patricia, Daniel; Mary and Kathleen; Marylin and Mary-Lee; Nadine and James; Nanci and Jeanne; Paul and

Robert; Paula, Laura and Sarah; Rae Ellen and Lois; Renee and Chick; Ronna and Dana; Rosemary and Sean; Sean and Kelly; Sherry and Jimmy; Sunny and Robert; Tami and Robert; Theresa and Eddie; Tracy and Debra; and Victoria and Susan.

May their stories of loss and courage give comfort to all who mourn.

Contents

Foreword

It's amazing that after more than fifty years of reflection upon the psychology of bereavement, there has been almost no attention to adult sibling loss. This omission is another glaring example of *disenfranchised loss* as described by Kenneth E. Doka. A disenfranchised loss is one that is not or cannot be openly acknowledged, publicly mourned, or socially accepted, such as the death of a same-sex partner or prenatal death. Other times, the mourner is not socially recognized—as often happens in the case of children, the elderly, and the mentally disabled. Until this study by T. J. Wray, the major significance of adult sibling loss had been ignored, forgotten, or trivialized. She has normalized the grief of adult siblings and empowered them to trust their own intuitions and to follow their natural inclinations on their journey toward healing.

Motivated by the death of her beloved brother when he was 43, Ms. Wray has explored and clarified almost every dimension of adult sibling loss. Drawing upon her own experiences of grief and those of hundreds of other grieving adult siblings, she has given social and psychological legitimacy to this type of bereavement. Lifting up adult sibling loss as having major consequences in the life of the sibling survivors, she has brought this type of death "out of the shadows . . . into the light of healing and hope." Because of her dedication, sensitivity, and insights, those who were often "the forgotten bereaved" are now more likely to be remembered, acknowledged, and cared for.

Ms. Wray has written an eminently practical and down-to-earth book addressed to all adults whose lives have been forever changed by the death of a brother or sister. In every chapter, she incorporates a variety of practical, proactive self-help suggestions highlighting both what helps those in grief and what generally doesn't. One suggestion I found empowering was her encouragement of mourners to recruit a grief partner to accompany the bereaved through his or her pilgrimage, someone who can offer empathy, compassion, and guidance on an ongoing basis and who can assist him or her to learn to live creatively without his or her sibling. I also appreciated her references to what she calls "dismissive condolences"—those words and actions from friends and acquaintances which, in trivializing the loss, do more harm than good. She has aided all of us to be more sensitive and in tune with mourners.

Another important contribution Ms. Wray makes is taking with utmost seriousness the impact of adult sibling loss upon the griever's religious life, particularly his or her views of the mercy and justice of God. She normalizes doubt and the loss of faith as a natural symptom of adult sibling loss and asserts that this symptom is usually transient and need not permanently estrange us from cherished religious convictions. As those in grief struggle with the meanings of the death of their adult sibling, they often rethink and modify their understandings of God and develop more mature religious commitments.

As one who has taught classes in bereavement for nearly twenty-five years, I welcome the illumination this book casts upon many forms of bereavement, not only adult sibling loss. Though focused on adult sibling loss, Ms. Wray has clarified the complex character of *all* grief. Although I have not lost an adult sibling, I have experienced the deaths of a spouse, parents, and close friends. To my surprise and satisfaction, I discovered that Ms. Wray's understanding of the bereavement of adult siblings captured and made sense out of my own struggles with grief and the gradual recovery of wholeness. This book is an invaluable and long overdue aid for anyone who has experienced a profound and painful loss, especially that of an adult sibling.

J. EARL THOMPSON
Guiles Professor of Pastoral Psychology
and Family Studies Emeritus
Andover Newton Theological School
Newton Centre, Massachusetts

SURVIVING

the DEATH of

a SIBLING

INTRODUCTION

Why a Book About Adult Sibling Grief?

The year my brother died, I forgot how to breathe.

Often it would catch me unaware, that terrible feeling that I was suffocating—at work, at home, sometimes at night, as I tried to sleep. As if I had drawn a breath but simply forgotten how to exhale. "I think there's something wrong with me," I confided one afternoon to a colleague who had also lost a sibling. "Sometimes, my chest aches," I told her. "Like I'm holding my breath for too long. I feel light-headed and weak and I'm so tired. My eyes water and I have trouble thinking clearly and talking." She was silent for a moment and then said quietly, "You're okay; it's just the grief." But I wasn't okay.

The year my brother died, I forgot how to breathe, and no one seemed to notice. Oh, they might have noticed a bit at first, but after a few weeks I could be walking around with my face turning blue and no one would say a word. After all, it was only my brother; I should get over it.

My *brother*. In the stillness of the early mornings when I have the house all to myself, I can recall his face and the sound of his voice so clearly that I'm often surprised, when I wake from my reverie, by his palpable absence. Even after five years, the shock of it all comes in bright, hot flashes and I blink back tears. I still hug my sides and rock back on my heels every now and then and ask, "Why?" Never expecting an answer. But most of all, I just miss him.

I miss our long conversations about religion and philosophy and how both can make people either enlightened or judgmental. I miss our deep belly laughs about our older sister Linda, and how as a skinny teenager she used to wear six slips under her skirt to make her butt look bigger. I miss making jokes about our mother's latest hair color, with both of us then feeling the same slightly guilty surge of love for her that only siblings can share. I miss my brother's honesty, and the way he could tell me that I was wrong without ever hurting my feelings simply because he knew me so well. I miss that familiar feeling that I have had all of my life: the comfort of simply knowing that he was in the world.

Memories of the early days and months following my brother's death are a mixture of people, feelings, and indistinct events jumbled together in the general swirl of grief. There is often a surreal feeling attached to those early memories, as if they had happened to someone else. There are also painfully vivid and detailed memories that jump out of the haze, like little vignettes, in which I appear as a person merely *playing* myself in some bizarre, terrible drama. I look back on my grieving self with great sadness, wishing that I could step back in time and offer her comfort. But that grieving me did not feel entitled to her grief and almost certainly would have rejected any overture. Indeed, within days of my brother's death I learned an important lesson. I learned that no matter how paralyzed with grief and sorrow I might have felt, society does not recognize the death of an adult brother or sister as a *major loss*. Comprehending this, I retreated into the shadows, a place where most other surviving brothers and sisters go to mourn, and waited for the sadness to pass.

• • •

My initial response to my brother's death was to search for information that would help me make sense of it all. I was certain that with the explosion of the Internet and online resources like Amazon.com, I'd be able to find books specifically addressing my situation. I was wrong. I searched the Internet for hours at a time, hoping to find something—be it a book or an article— that might help me to better understand and cope with my grief. And I spent long afternoons prowling the stacks at our local library and the university library near my home. But those searches were always in vain.

For while I located countless books, articles, and self-help tapes intended to help the bereaved in coping with the death of a parent, a spouse, or a child (and, much to my surprise, even uncovered a wealth of information dealing with the subject of pet loss), I was amazed to find that there was virtually nothing written on the subject of adult sibling grief. How could this be? More than 2.5 million deaths occur in the United States each year, meaning that roughly 4.2 million adult siblings experience the death of a brother or a sister. Why, then, was there nothing written by the so-called grief experts to help all of those surviving siblings cope with such a difficult loss? Surely there must be others, I reasoned, who felt as I did—that the death of a brother or a sister was a major, life-changing event.

In view of this dearth of material, I felt a special need to connect with other surviving siblings who might understand my grief. I hoped that they could offer me some insight, some comfort, some practical advice that might help me through those first difficult weeks and months. How had *they* survived this? There must be some special formula, some secret that I didn't know about. And so I investigated grief support groups; various special lectures for the newly bereaved offered by churches, funeral homes, and therapists; and online forums dealing with grief and loss. But none of these specifically addressed the subject of adult sibling grief. I recall one particularly painful phone call I made to a bereavement group I had read about in our local newspaper. "Is there anyone in the group who has lost a sibling?" I asked the elderly woman who took my phone call. "A sibling?" she asked. "No, dear, this is an adult group." I hung up the phone, strangely embarrassed and ashamed for acting so "childish."

Indeed, the only information concerning sibling loss that I *was* able to unearth was geared almost exclusively toward young children. Not that those resources aren't necessary and pertinent (losing a sibling at any age is a devastating event), but I recall asking myself, "Are we suddenly expected to stop caring for our siblings once we enter adulthood?" After all, the endless resources available to aid youngsters in dealing with the death of a sibling indicate the importance of the sibling relationship in shaping our lives. And why would this initial relationship lose any significance as it ripened into adulthood? Wouldn't it render itself only more important (and certainly more complex) than it had been to start with?

The sad fact is this: When an adult loses a brother or a sister, society often fails to recognize the depth of such a loss. Witness what I call *dismissive condolences*, offered by well-intentioned but sorely misguided friends, acquaintances, family members, and coworkers: "Well, you lived in different states, so you probably weren't very close." Or "Thank goodness it wasn't your husband or one of your children." And "Your brother/sister died? How awful! How are your *parents*?" Intellectually, we may understand that people mean well; they're attempting to be helpful and to offer comfort to us in our sorrow. Yet dismissive condolences have the opposite effect. They make our loss seem trivial, and they also make the surviving sibling feel as if his or her grief is somehow unwarranted.

I myself was the recipient of countless dismissive condolences from perfectly caring, well-intentioned folks, and while some acknowledgment was welcomed (at least they made an attempt to recognize my grief), I began to wonder if my grief response was perhaps inappropriate. Was I overreacting? After all, my brother and I *did* live in different states, I *was* thankful that my husband and children were alive, and my parents *were* completely unraveled by their loss. Maybe I wasn't behaving as a grieving person should behave. But I had never lost anyone so close to me before. How long was I supposed to feel sad? Was my behavior abnormal? I had no idea.

I now realize that the reason I was so frustrated with my inability to "get over it" was due, in part, to my acceptance of the message sent to me by society and the grief experts. This message, conveyed by silence, apathy, or ignorance, was that my grief was somehow less important than others'. I now understand, however, that my feelings were normal, healthy reactions to the death of someone who had been part of my life since the day I was born. And I also know now that even though surviving adult siblings certainly share many of the grief reactions associated with other kinds of loss, there are some significant differences—differences rooted in the distinctive nature of a relationship, which, unlike any other relationship, begins in childhood and continues into old age.

· · ·

When an adult sibling dies before his or her parents, the remaining siblings must not only deal with their own grief; they must also help their parents cope with losing a child, precisely when they may be least equipped to help anyone. The fact is, surviving brothers and sisters, more often than not, need their parents to help *them*. This can result in feelings of isolation and disconnectedness just when the opposite is required. Surviving siblings usually end up feeling selfish and guilty for not being better sons or daughters to their grieving parents, repressing their own grief in a halfhearted effort to help their parents.

The entire family structure is forever altered by the death of one of its members. Roles we've had for a lifetime are suddenly tossed in the air like so many Pick Up sticks, and the subsequent scramble to find a new place within the family is often a difficult adjustment. A middle child may suddenly become the eldest or the youngest in the family, for instance.

The sibling relationship is more complex than nearly any other, a mixture of affection and ambivalence, camaraderie and competition. Aside from your parents, there is simply no one else on earth who knows you better, because, like your parents, your brothers and sisters have been beside you from the very beginning. Unlike your parents, however, your siblings are people you assume will be part of your life for the *rest* of your life, too. In terms of the span of time, the intimacy, and the shared experience of childhood, no other relationship rivals the connection we have with our adult brothers or sisters. From schoolyard bullies to teenage broken hearts, from careers to marriage to dreams unfulfilled, our siblings have been there through it all, life partners in our journey through time. They are the keepers of secrets, perennial rivals for our parents' affections, and a secure and familiar constant in an often precarious and uncertain world.

While all families are unique and different (we all have our secrets, crazy relatives, embarrassing stories, and wonderful, magical moments), only your brothers and sisters know firsthand what it was like to grow up in your particular family. Only they are able to view family life through such a similar lens. Sure, my siblings may have different reactions to and interpretations of the same event, but the fact remains, *they were there*. Although each child is an individual member of a family, he or she is also part of a larger circle—a circle that helps to define who we are and provides a link to our shared past. Losing a sibling, then, can also mean losing a part of yourself, part of that special connection to the past. How do we learn to live with the broken circle that is now our family?

• • •

Although for years I'd been teaching a course that deals with the complex issues of death, dying, and the grief process, I felt ill prepared to cope with losing my only brother. I quickly learned that understanding the process of grief, in the intellectual sense, doesn't matter very much when you are knee deep in tears. And I knew that in order to heal and to learn to live within that broken circle, I needed to stop concealing my grief and begin reaching out to others.

As I began to speak more openly about this topic, I found that there were countless cases of unresolved grief among other surviving siblings, and I soon reached the conclusion that adult sibling bereavement is what psychologists call a *disenfranchised loss*, which in simple terms means that society fails to classify our mourning as a legitimate loss. After all, when an adult sibling dies, he or she often leaves behind parents, a spouse, and even children—all of whom suffer a more socially recognized loss. As one bereaved sibling put it, "How could I go into mourning when I had my brother's wife and children to take care of, not to mention my parents? I can't recall anyone ever asking me how I felt during that time." The purpose of this book, therefore, is to lend comfort and support to surviving adult siblings. Those who have contributed to this book did so with the sole desire to help others tread the muddy waters of sibling loss—waters through which they themselves have already passed. This is not a psychoanalytic book. Nor is it intended to replace any form of grief therapy or psychological counseling, though it may serve to complement either.

Dr. Elisabeth Kübler-Ross was among the first to describe the process of dying in terms of stages. These stages also correspond to the grief process: stage one—shock, denial, and isolation; stage two—anger; stage three—bargaining; stage four—depression; and stage five—acceptance. But while Kübler-Ross maintained that it seems there are discernible stages through which a dying/grieving person passes, she also recognized that these stages are by no means fixed or universal. In other words, one may pass quickly or slowly through a particular stage; pass through stages "out of order" or not at all; pass through one stage only to slip back into that stage at a later date; and so forth.

Since Kübler-Ross's initial work, many others have put forth their own models in an effort to describe the complex process of grieving. According to grief and bereavement author Earl Grollman, each person's grief journey is as unique as a fingerprint or a snowflake. This begs the question: If the process of grief is so individual and complex, why do we need a model at all? The truth is, many modern psychological theorists reject the use of stages or models in describing this highly individual process. I've found, however, that even those theorists who jettison the use of models in describing grief usually end up stringing together many of the universal reactions to loss into essentially nonstructured models. While I wholeheartedly concur with the notion of grief as an individual process and understand it to be a normal, healthy response to the death of a loved one (and, in most cases, not pathological), I have come to believe that models, to a very limited degree, can be helpful.

Models, at the very least, provide a framework that enables us to understand grief as a *process*. In fact, when I initially began to gather information from surviving siblings, I used a twelve-page questionnaire framed around Kübler-Ross's well-delineated model. Why? The answer is more practical than theoretical. In my many conversations with grieving siblings, Kübler-Ross's work was the only work ever referenced. The average person may not be aware of recent shifts in grief therapy or arguments about the pros and cons of models, but most have some knowledge of Kübler-Ross. And this book is for the average person, rather than for the clinician.

Further, because Kübler-Ross's model lends itself naturally to an easy-to-read, understandable framework that proceeds in a clear, logical fashion, I decided to use it as a starting point. Her descriptions of certain grief reactions—particularly shock, denial, anger, depression, and acceptance—have become chapters in this book because they accurately describe my own grief journey, and the journey of many others as well.

I've tried to be mindful of the fact that most grieving persons lack the energy or interest to sift through lengthy essays or psychological analyses, preferring a simple, straightforward approach—one right from the horse's mouth, so to speak. Although this book is best read from cover to cover, I've arranged the chapters so that the reader is able to glance at the table of contents and locate quickly the chapter or chapters most pertinent to his or her particular place in the grief process. The smaller, prescriptive sections that conclude each chapter ("What Helps") reinforce the core of the chapters and offer the reader practical and proactive self-help suggestions.

In addition to this book, I would suggest that readers visit our website: www.adultsiblinggrief.com. This site features general information, a message board, chat rooms, and other helpful features tailored specifically for surviving adult siblings.

Finally, I did not write this book alone. The stories of other surviving siblings, who so selflessly shared their experiences in order to help others, proved to be a great source of comfort to me on the days when writing was most difficult, and for this I am most humbly grateful. It is my sincere hope that our collective effort will bring this most important and neglected type of grief out of the shadows and into the light of healing and hope.

On behalf of all those who have contributed to this effort, and in loving memory of all of the siblings whose lives are herein memorialized, I wish you peace.

1

SHOCK

Dealing with the News

*We brothers and sisters were so happy at home. . . .
Who could have then believed that life would ever
become so torn asunder—*

—DAG HAMMARSKJÖLD

THE OLD beige afghan rests silently on the top shelf, carefully buried beneath all the other blankets. Each time I open the large closet in the hallway outside my bedroom, I know it's there, patiently waiting. Over the years, I've learned to open and close the closet door quickly, replacing and fetching towels or blankets with practiced precision. My eyes know better than to sneak a glance upward; it's dangerous, that afghan. There have been times, however, when that old shawl, lonely and tired of being ignored, exerts its power over me. I feel its pull, like a seductive whisper; I reach up and touch the fringes that dangle like fingers over the edge of the shelf, and I remember. The tears come then—the great rolling tears of grief, and the afghan is appeased, at least for a time.

Thinking back to that terrible January day is still difficult for me. What I remember most is the cold. I see myself sitting on the couch and shivering as the icy New England wind slices through the seams of our drafty old house. Unable to keep warm, I wrap myself in the shabby comfort of the old afghan my grandmother gave me on my wedding day. I gaze at the blackened fireplace, too weary to start a fire, too miserable to be cheered by it. I am waiting for a phone call. All around me, there's an unnatural silence, the kind of silence that rings. Except for the dogs, Katie and India, who sleep curled up next to each other on the doggy bed in the kitchen, I am alone. In a house that boasts three children, two dogs, and a husband who speaks to everyone as if they are hard of hearing, there is now quiet.

My family waited with me earlier in the morning, speaking in hushed, overly articulated voices, closing doors deliberately, and padding about the house in socks. Even my husband whispered as he ushered the dogs in and out of the back door. After several hours, however, their voices began to grow louder and I became agitated. Inquiring heads poked into the living room and I shot back quick, dismissive frowns. Thankfully, my husband suddenly decided a trip to the drugstore was in order. I knew my family was eager to get away from the drama unfolding around us, and I couldn't blame them; I wanted to escape, too. As they bundled into coats and mittens, I was both glad and terrified at the prospect of being left alone. They bolted from the back door like prisoners on a furlough, and quickly climbed into the bitter comfort of the car. I watched from the window as they drove off, returning the wave of my youngest child, Jack, who flapped both red mittens at me through the frosty rear window.

Slowly, I return to my station on the couch and gaze outside at the trees bending stiffly to the wind. I decide that the cold is somehow appropriate. This day *should* be cold. I sit for a long time, unmoving, and my back begins to ache. I stretch and then look over at the cordless phone on the coffee table, instinctively knowing it's about to ring. Seconds later, it does. The ring, like a scream, still manages to startle me and a rush of adrenaline sends pinpricks down my arms. A small voice inside me warns, "Don't answer," but I ignore the voice. I press the blue button on the receiver and say, "Hello?" My older sister Robin is on the other end. "It's me," she says, by way of a greeting. Then, quietly and evenly, she tells me, "It's over. He's gone." I look at my watch. It's 11:20 A.M. Thoughts race through my head. I open my mouth to say something, and then close it. A wave of nausea passes over me and I put a hand on my stomach—and then to my mouth. I notice that my hand is shaking and realize that my knees are trembling, too.

I look about the room, as if someone will appear to help me. I swallow and then whisper, "Oh my God, Robin, what are we going to do?" She makes no response, and I can tell she's crying.

I want to tell my sister not to cry, that everything will be all right, but I know, in those first few moments following my brother's death, that nothing will ever be all right again. My sister continues to cry softly, and I'm unable to move. I now understand the meaning of the phrase "paralyzed with grief." Abruptly, I cough and gulp air; without realizing it, I've been holding my breath. "Are you okay?" my sister asks, concerned. "Yes. I'm fine," I say. "I just stopped breathing for a minute." I don't mean for my reply to be funny, but under the circumstances, in some macabre way, it is. We don't exactly laugh, though—just groan simultaneously. For a moment, I feel comforted in the familiarity of this. Then another silence. Time passes. It seems like several minutes, though it's probably no more than a few seconds. I know that we should hang up the phone and do something (but what?), yet neither of us seems able to end the connection. Finally, I say, "I'd better go now." My sister sniffs miserably and says, "Me, too. I'll call you tomorrow." Then she is gone.

I sit for a long time, staring at the cordless phone in my hand. I shake my head slowly in disbelief and then curl up into a tiny ball on the couch and cover my body, including my head, with the old afghan. I decide to remain there for the rest of my life.

Soon, my husband and children return from the drugstore, their voices gathering on the front steps and becoming a burst of noise and frenzy as they tumble through the door into the kitchen. The dogs are roused and they dance a greeting, their nails clicking on the slippery pine floor. Boots are kicked off, a bag rustles, dogs are spoken to in baby talk. Under the afghan, I bristle at the invasion. Abruptly, there is silence; the dogs return to their bed without command. Something about the house has changed, and my family senses it. They walk quietly into the living room and stand in front of the heap on the couch. No one says a word. It's 11:30 A.M. Ten minutes have passed since the phone call, but it is as if the world itself has passed away while my family shopped for razor blades and a newspaper.

Of course, I eventually crawl out from under the afghan, but the rest of that day is just a blur. I carry the afghan around with me for weeks, a child and her blankie; I sleep under it and seek it out after work like a consoling friend. It becomes my mantle in grief, and no one else dares touch it.

The initial shock and numbness I feel quickly gives way to an overwhelming sense of disbelief and the creepy, eerie sensation that I am no longer confined to my body. It's as if I'm watching everything happen to someone who looks like me but who cannot possibly *be* me. Later, as I wander from room to room in my house whispering "Oh my God. Oh my God. Oh my God" I'm certain I must be losing my mind.

Today, however, looking back, I understand that I was in shock and that feeling numb or paralyzed is a perfectly normal grief reaction. Other surviving siblings, like Carl, have felt similarly.

> *I was driving my car and my brother, Greg [age 29], was a pas-senger. I fell asleep at the wheel and hit a telephone pole. Neither of us was wearing a seat belt and though I escaped with minor injuries, Greg was killed instantly. I was in a state of shock for several hours. I understood what had happened, but my emotions were on hold. I was in the hospital with a broken arm. It was only when I saw a priest (some four hours after the accident) talking with my doctor did I suspect that Greg had died. Still, no emotions came to me until my mother came to see me and we all cried together. Another wave hit me when I saw Greg's body at the funeral home. It was cold and lifeless and pale, and this made the loss feel more real.* —CARL, 29

Although Carl and I share comparable initial reactions upon hearing the news of our brothers' deaths, these reactions are by no means universal. I suppose, on an intuitive level, I understood that right from the start. After all, my sister Robin had a quite different reaction when she called to deliver the news of my brother's death. She cried as she told me about my brother, even as I found myself unable to. Each of us will react differently to the news of a brother's or a sister's death, and there's hardly a *standard of behavior* to which we must all subscribe.

How we react to the news is largely determined by the differences in our particular personalities, of course, but there are other contributing factors to consider as well. For example, were you alone, as I was, when you received the news? How was the news delivered to you (and by whom)? Where exactly were you when you heard the news? At home? At work? How much support did you receive in the hours following the news? Was your sibling's death anticipated or sudden? What was the nature of your relationship with your sibling before his or her death? These and other factors influence the impact of shock. Janet, who was at work when she received the news of her brother's death, offers a detailed description of her reaction and captures many of the feelings often associated with shock.

The office manager and one of my coworkers told me together that someone had called from a hospital in California to notify me that my brother, Jim [age 54], had been critically injured in a car accident. It was apparent that both of them were standing by to support me. My own reaction was disbelief. My brother doesn't have serious accidents, I reminded myself. He isn't a reckless risk-taker. This is not possible. Maybe this was a case of mistaken identity? I called the number the office manager had given me and reached a nurse in the trauma unit. After I had identified myself, she proceeded to describe all of my brother's injuries. It took her a very long time, and I was somewhere between stunned and unbelieving. The office manager took over, perceiving that I was essentially nonfunctional, and made airline reserva-

tions for me (she later picked me up and drove me to the air-
port). I was unable to focus and my mind was spinning crazily.
— JANET, 57

Other reactions to the shocking news of a sister's or a brother's death include feelings of confusion or disorientation. Many surviving siblings report that they were unable to think clearly, yet they had the presence of mind to focus sharply on a particular task at hand, like packing a suitcase or making plane reservations. A strange sense that time seems to stand still is also fairly common, as well as a pervasive feeling of not knowing what to do. I felt this way myself soon after receiving the news of my brother's death; there was a nagging sense that I needed to do something, but I was unable to quiet my mind long enough to figure out just what it was.

Much of early grief is fundamentally a visceral reaction. This means that in addition to the obvious emotional reactions associated with shock, you may also experience a variety of physical symptoms. These symptoms range from the relatively mild, such as the shakiness I felt, to the more severe, such as feeling as if you are going to faint, like Nadine did.

My mother left to pick up my brother at his new apartment for a
prearranged dinner date. She had been somewhat anxious because
she had been unable to reach him by phone all day. An hour
later, I answered the incessant pounding at the front door to find
two policemen who were practically carrying my mother. They
informed me that my brother was "deceased." My mother cried
out that James [age 29] had killed himself. I felt as if every drop
of blood had drained from my body. I thought I was going to
pass out. — NADINE, 41

Other physical reactions of shock include stomach disorders, ranging from the kind of nausea that assailed me to a more severe clutching sensation in the stomach. Some surviving siblings experience shortness of breath, dizziness, general weakness, and even an inability to speak. Others may complain of chest pain, and a few may fear they're going to have a heart attack and die themselves. In fact, it's quite common for surviving siblings to develop physical symptoms that may at least *seem* life threatening. Before experiencing the death of a brother or a sister, we might have dismissed such symptoms as psychosomatic, but now anything seems possible. As one surviving sibling put it, "The veil of safety has been lifted with the death of a sibling. If your sibling can die suddenly, then so can you."

I was always startled by late-night phone calls because I feared hearing that my alcoholic younger brother had been in an accident. The call came in the middle of the day as I was teaching high school. My mother barely spoke; she mostly groaned and gasped. I asked if Andy [age 22] was hurt. She said, "Yes." I remember the brashness I felt as I asked if he was dead. It almost felt like a profanity passing over my lips. Instantly, I felt the cold brick wall slam into my back. My pregnant stomach began a series of violent spasms, which I feared was killing my baby. I will never forget how cold that wall felt or how much I feared that my grief would harm my unborn baby.

—LISA-MARIE, 34

While it's true that we all react to tragic news in our own way, the cause of death often determines much of our shock reaction. In my case, I knew ahead of time that my brother was dying. He had been critically ill for a little over a week, and I had spent much of that time with him. He was living in Florida, so I left my husband and children at home in Providence and flew to Orlando, along with my sisters and my mother. Although I had not known that he would die from his illness before I left Providence, after a day and a half, there was little doubt that his condition was indeed terminal. I remained in Florida until he slipped into an irreversible coma, and then, unable emotionally to endure the circumstances any longer, I left. This decision to leave him has haunted me for years, and I suspect that it always will; but at the time, it seemed like the only way to hold on to my sanity.

When I got on the plane to fly home, I knew that my brother was going to die. His death, then, can be classified as an *anticipated death*. Naturally, the shock response associated with an anticipated death, as in the case of my brother's death or any other type of terminal illness, is likely to differ from the shock response resulting from a sudden, *unanticipated death*, as in the cases previously mentioned.

This is not to say that one death is any more tragic than another, only that the shock reaction of surviving siblings is probably going to be different based on the manner in which their sibling died. If you know that your brother or sister is dying, you will likely begin to grieve for your sibling in anticipation of his or her death. You may even have the opportunity to resolve differences, ask for or offer forgiveness, or tell your sibling how much you love him or her. Clearly, having the chance to express your feelings while your brother or sister is dying can be beneficial, both to your dying sibling and, most of all, to you.

In many cases, the illness allows you to gradually prepare for the inevitable. Learning that your sibling is suffering from a terminal condition, however, brings a unique type of shock—in effect, something of a *double whammy*. In other words, you may end up grieving for your brother or sister *twice:* first when the reality of the prognosis has been accepted, and then again following your sibling's death, as in Laura's case.

I passed through the first stage [shock, denial, isolation] when I found out about Sarah's [age 36] illness. She was diagnosed with lung cancer and died just eight weeks later. During that eight-week period, I went through all of the stages, and started a sec-

ond round after Sarah died. The shock did not return, though, when Sarah died. I had prepared myself for her death.

—LAURA, 39

For Laura, the shock was not as acute following Sarah's death as it was when she found out that her sister was dying. But many surviving siblings report the reverse. Even when we try to convince ourselves that we're somehow prepared for the eventual death of our critically ill sibling, the reality is often the opposite. For example, I had a little over a week to prepare myself for my brother's death, and in many ways I thought that I *was* prepared. My response to his death, however, indicates that this was not the case. There seems to be a connection, however tenuous, between the amount of time surviving siblings have to prepare themselves for their brother's or sister's death and the manner in which they process the actual news of their sibling's passing, as illustrated in Julianne's story.

I received a phone call on Wednesday evening, just as I was getting ready to go to class. My brother, Scott [age 32], had gone into the hospital that Monday because of breathing problems, which everyone assumed were due to pneumonia, developing from the flu he seemed to have had for two or three weeks. So I wasn't surprised that my mother was calling with news, but when she told me that he had lung cancer—lung cancer—all I could say was "What?" over and over. He was thirty-two years old and a nonsmoker. How could he have lung cancer? It turned out that it was metastatic from testicular cancer and was so advanced that he died that Saturday, after receiving only one dose of chemo. We were with him when he died, fortunately, because, as hard as that is, it would have been much harder not to have been with him at the end. The first thing I remember thinking when the nurse said it was over was "I wish the world would just open up right now and swallow everything."

—JULIANNE, 40

Some surviving siblings, like Julianne, are actually with their brother or sister at the time of death, and most consider this to be very meaningful. It's an honor to share those last few moments of life with your brother or sister, and most surviving brothers and sisters believe that being present at the time of death helps them to better deal with their loss. My oldest sister, Linda, who is four years older than my brother, said, "I was there when he came into the world and I was there when he left; his big sister to the very end."

If, on the other hand, you're denied the chance to be with your dying brother or sister, for whatever reason, then you'll probably have a much more difficult time when you learn of his or her death. You are likely to feel, as I do, that you missed the opportunity to be with your sibling as he or she left this world, and you'll probably suffer a great deal of sadness and regret because of it. I knew when I stepped onto the plane in Orlando to return home that I had made a huge mistake in leaving my brother. The plane was filled with happy families in Mickey Mouse ears and Goofy T-shirts—the smiling, sunburned faces of the Disney World experience. But I sat slumped in my seat, head against the window, feeling like a traitor. The excited chatter of children reliving their moments on Splash Mountain only heightened my desolation, which I accepted as penance for my desertion.

Another important factor in determining how you might deal with the shocking news that your brother or sister has died has to do with the meaning we attach to death and mourning; in other words, grief behavior is often learned and directly relates to an individual's worldview. Our religion (or lack thereof), our culture, our past losses, even our gender can influence the manner in which we receive the news and our subsequent grief response.

For people of my generation, a commonly asked question is "Where were you when President Kennedy was shot?" I was not quite five years old when Kennedy was killed, and I had no clear sense of who he was. Nonetheless, his death remains my earliest memory of grief. What I recall with striking clarity is my mother's reaction. When she returned home from work, she seemed very sad and quiet, and I knew immediately that something was terribly wrong. She went directly into the bathroom and closed the door. I stationed myself just outside on the steps leading upstairs and waited in the darkness for her to come out. After a few moments, I heard the muffled sounds of her crying. Bewildered and afraid, I sat there frozen, listening to the sounds of my mother's grief. I cried, too, that night, but not for the president. I wept for the person I loved most in the world, who at that very moment sat alone in our tiny pink bathroom, sobbing into a towel in hopes of silencing her grief.

I would not recall this memory in detail until over thirty years later, when I sat alone on the floor of my own bathroom, pouring out my shock and grief over the death of my only brother into a towel, silently praying that my young children would not hear.

The suppressed, hidden manner in which I initially grieved for my brother was a learned behavior. But this behavior is hardly unusual, especially for surviving brothers and sisters. Often conscripted to the shadows in our time of sorrow, surviving siblings rarely feel they have the right to grieve beyond a few weeks. In a society that doesn't always encourage healthy mourning in general, we are indeed the *forgotten bereaved*.

Of course, most Americans have an evasive attitude when it comes to any issues surrounding death and bereavement. This may seem somewhat ridiculous, considering that we will all experience the death of a loved one at some point in life, but for most Americans, talk about death and loss simply makes them feel uncomfortable. In fact, there's an expectation of stoicism in the face of grief, and the less you allow the death of a loved one to affect you, the stronger you are perceived to be. Such "inner strength in the face of adversity" becomes not only admirable, but de rigueur. I have found, however, that what often seems like stoicism may not be stoicism at all. "Bearing up well" or "handling one's grief" may simply be examples of shock, as in the case of Renee.

> *I was out with a friend for dinner one evening. When I returned home, there were several calls on my answering machine. My two daughters, a friend, and my brother's [Chick, 68] wife had all called and left similar messages. They all wanted me to call them back immediately, at any hour. I just knew. My daughters and their husbands came to my house to be with me, and they all thought that I was being wonderfully stoic; but in reality, I was just in shock and disbelief. That same feeling still comes up for me even after four and a half years.* —RENEE, 69

As a society, we need to question the effectiveness of this attitude. I strongly believe that "ignoring it" so that it will go away or "handling it" only leads to repressed grief, which brings with it all sorts of additional problems, including depression and an inability to deal with future losses.

Two years before my brother died, I worked as a teacher in a large, all-female Catholic high school. One day, shortly after the beginning of the second semester, the unthinkable happened: One of our students, a beautiful senior with her whole life and future ahead of her, committed suicide. The students were understandably shaken, and the faculty, including me, wondered if there had been clues we might have missed that could have prevented this tragedy. The young woman who took her life was Hispanic, and I will never forget the reactions of her family during the wake and funeral. Family members grieved openly, crying, wailing, and falling to the floor, overcome with shock and disbelief. Most of the young, non-Hispanic students who witnessed this type of grief were surprised, and some of them were even fearful. Although I had warned many of them earlier in the day about the various cultural responses to death, most of them still felt out of place and uncomfortable with this open display of shock and sorrow.

Driving home from the wake that afternoon, I cried in the car for the lovely young woman whose family had mourned so deeply for her, and my heart ached for their loss. I also felt that in many ways, her family's way of grieving was probably more psychologically beneficial than the way most Americans grieve.

• • •

In my conversations with surviving siblings, I have noticed recurrent *themes of grief*. For instance, one of the most prevalent aspects of shock, mentioned by nearly all of the surviving siblings with whom I spoke, was an overwhelming sense of despair. Dean captures this feeling best in his story of Stefani's sudden death.

It was a Saturday morning and Stefani [age 25] hadn't come home Friday night, which was very unusual for her. While I tried to locate her, a friend of hers called to tell me there was an article in the morning newspaper about an unidentified woman jogger in her twenties being fatally struck by a truck at 6:00 P.M. the previous night near our house. Stefani was a regular jogger, and I immediately feared that she was the victim. My brother and I raced to the police station, where an officer met us with a Polaroid photograph of the victim. It was Stefani. My first reaction was to deny that it was her in the photograph. I said, "The face is too swollen to tell." But I knew it was her. I then went into absolute despair. This was too horrible and terrible to be true. It was simply too catastrophic to deal with. I was older than Stefani by just eleven months. We'd grown up like twins, and I had always felt very protective of my sister. Stefani being dead so suddenly was an overload of terror that was simply too great to process mentally or emotionally. I felt my mind, my entire self, shut down and go totally numb with despair. I went through the next couple of weeks on autopilot, incapable of really processing or acknowledging the full weight of Stefani's death.

—DEAN, 30

According to statistics from the National Safety Council, accidents claim the lives of one American every six minutes. It's not surprising, then, that many surviving siblings are forced to cope with the difficult grief associated with sudden death, shattering their false notions of security in a world that is far from predictable. Sudden deaths rob us of the chance to offer comfort to our siblings in their final moments of life, to tell our siblings all of those things that lie deep within our souls, whether untold childhood secrets or disappointments over unfulfilled grown-up dreams. They deprive us of the chance to ask for or to offer forgiveness for whatever childhood (or adult) transgressions may have passed between us. They take from us the final good-bye that can be so helpful in healthy grieving, leaving us with words forever left unsaid.

I had heard on the news that there was a landslide at a popular waterfall. My sister, Donna [age 38], asked me if there was a waterfall she and her husband could see on the island. After hearing the news about the landslide, my boyfriend and I drove to the parking lot of this scenic attraction. I saw their rented car. I knew they were there. I felt dread and panic, but did not know for sure. The longer the search took, the more dread I felt. After I found Donna's husband in the critical care unit, I realized something horrible must have happened to my sister. It wasn't until the next morning when I received the call from the medical examiner that I knew for certain. I remember he said, "This is Frank from the Medical Examiner's Office. I understand that you are looking for someone." It was then that I knew that the worst had happened. My first reaction was shock, but also relief. I did not want to think of my sister being cold, scared, or suffering.

Not knowing was the worst part. Her death was fairly sudden. The rocks fell on Donna and Mike. Her lower body was crushed. Someone found Donna with her eyes wide open, still breathing, but with difficulty. A kind stranger picked her up and carried her to a safer place. He held her hand and talked to her and tried to comfort her as she lay dying. She said that her name was Donna and that she was having trouble breathing. This kind stranger told her that she was breathing fine and to listen to the sound of the waterfall and the wind blowing through the leaves. He tried to keep her talking while they waited for help to arrive. She told the stranger to tell her husband, Mike, that she loved him. I guess she finally passed thirty-five to forty-five minutes after the rocks fell. Informing my parents before they heard it on CNN was heart wrenching. —DARCEY, 37*

Another type of death that often takes siblings by surprise is *catastrophic death*, in which a sudden illness, such as meningitis or a heart attack, results in death. An illness may start out as seemingly routine—for instance, a nasty cold, upset stomach, or sudden fatigue—only to escalate and become more serious. We may or may not have been informed that our sibling has been ill, particularly if we live some distance away and are not in the habit of communicating on a regular basis. If your brother or sister dies due to a sudden, catastrophic illness you didn't even know about, you may later feel a great deal of guilt and regret for not keeping in better touch with your sibling. In fact, one survivor told me that she felt responsible for her brother's death: "I'm his sister. If I had called him or visited him more often, I would have been able to tell that he was ill. I know him better than anyone."

But the truth is, it's not uncommon for adult siblings to have a somewhat unconventional or sporadic mode of communication with one another. It doesn't seem to matter whether we've remained in close contact with our sibling, or whether months have passed since our last conversation; the connection forged in childhood is a lifelong bond that somehow endures. How many other relationships in our lives could withstand weeks or months of silence? The truth about sibling relationships is that no matter how old we become, how much we may change, how far away we may wander, or how infrequently we may communicate, we're forever connected. This is an unspoken truth that lives in the heart of every sister and brother.

On the other hand, you may have maintained a close relationship with your brother or sister, like Helen and JoAnn. Although JoAnn had been feeling poorly for a few days, Helen was not unusually alarmed.

My brother-in-law, Bill, called me shortly after my sister, JoAnn [age 54], died suddenly. She had not been ill, but had been feeling poorly for a couple of days and had been in bed. He had called earlier that day to ask me if I could come down and stay with JoAnn the next day (forty-five miles away) while he ran errands. Bill felt uncomfortable leaving JoAnn alone. That night, as my husband and I were sleeping, Bill called to tell me that JoAnn had died late that evening (from heart failure). My reaction was to go into shock, and then despair. I almost didn't know how to feel. My world had suddenly turned into some weird, alien place, and I felt very uncomfortable just living, as if life were some strange, bad movie, with an inexplicable ending. I was as close to my sister (my only sibling) as I am to anyone in my life, with the possible exception of my husband. Losing her without having the chance to prepare for her death or the opportunity to say good-bye causes me unbearable grief to this day.

—HELEN, 46

Sibling deaths due to sudden illness, like JoAnn's, are shocking because they are so unexpected. Even though it may be clear that nothing could have been done to save your brother or sister, many survivors nonetheless experience regret over not having recognized possible signs of an impending catastrophic event. You might beat yourself up for not pushing harder for your brother or sister to see a doctor, or you might feel guilty for not being more strident in expressing concerns to your sibling about certain behaviors (such as the sister who is overweight and smokes constantly) that may have contributed to a fatal outcome. In either case, this particular type of unanticipated death is exceptionally difficult to process, and the emotion experienced by surviving siblings can best be described as *stunned*.

> *I will never forget the day of my brother's death. My 18-year-old son told me the news: "One of your brothers died." My mind whirled. I could feel the blood leaving my face while flashes of my older brother, an overweight smoker, collapsing on the handball court raced through my mind. But it wasn't my older brother; nor was it my brother the high-stressed banker. It was Sean [age 43]. A lifetime passed. Oh no! Sean! Not Sean! The fear and terror of that moment is still with me at times. The death was so sudden, a heart attack, after playing squash at the Officers' Club. What helped me through the first twenty-four hours was the knowledge that my remaining three brothers, my parents, and I would be flying to the East Coast to be with Sean's widow and his six children, whom we hadn't seen in two years. I guess I just put one foot in front of the other during those first few hours. I told a complete stranger on the plane our family story and all about Sean's life. She didn't know what to say.*
>
> —ROSEMARY, 51

· · ·

It's three o'clock in the morning and all at once you're awake and fully alert. You stare into the darkness for a few moments trying to figure out just what it was that disturbed your sleep. Was it a bad dream? A strange sound? Still confused, you're suddenly filled with dread. *Why?* Suddenly, the phone rings. Before you even answer the call, you're certain the person on the other end is the harbinger of bad news. It's been less than ten seconds since you first opened your eyes, but once you pick up that phone, your life will forever be changed, and you'll never be the same person you were just a few moments ago.

> *I still remember waking early that morning, around 4:00 A.M. Several minutes later, the phone rang. A hospital spokesman asked to speak with my dad. He and my mother were asked to come to the hospital. I remember feeling deep down inside that my brother, Robert [age 26], had been killed. Several hours later, that feeling was confirmed.* —PAUL, 38

Some siblings, like Paul, report that they had had a premonition, or an intuition, that something had happened to their sibling before actually hearing the news. This is particularly true of twins, who often report strange phenomena, such as one twin feeling a sharp pain in the chest at the very moment the other twin suffers a heart attack some three thousand miles away.

> *When Bryan [age 28], my identical twin brother, didn't show up for our softball game, I knew something was wrong. He hadn't missed a game with me in twenty-two years. Later that night I received the call, and that's when I knew he was gone.* —BRAD, 40

Though we most often hear of these unusual connections between twins, many other siblings report similar experiences, such as receiving a phone call from your brother just as you were going to the phone to call him, or opening a Christmas gift from your sister only to find that it's the exact gift you've given to her. All of these are examples of what I like to call the *sibling sixth sense.* I have experienced this sixth sense with nearly all of my siblings, but most notably with my brother. On countless occasions, the phone would ring in my hand just as I was about to call him.

Other siblings report this phenomenon, but few take it very seriously. "It's just part of being a sibling. We can sense things," my own sister tells me. "What's so unusual about that?" I smile, knowing that it *is* a remarkable thing, and even more remarkable that we take it for granted.

> *My younger brother, Andy [age 27], had been missing for about a week, but he was a grown man and we just figured that he'd taken off on an impulse to go camping at Yosemite, Baja, or another of his favorite getaway places. The timing struck me as odd, however, because his grapevines were like cherished children to him, and his leaving so close to harvesttime seemed strange. One afternoon, my mother called to ask if I had heard anything from him yet, and she went on to speak of other people she had contacted, including his AA sponsor. I had a sudden moment of stunned, wooden disbelief. Then everything seemed to stop and heave around me. It was as if a wall of blackness hit my face. I went cold and numb all over. I could not swallow or breathe, because I knew, without a doubt, that Andy was dead, that he had killed himself, that his body was somewhere in Adobe Gulch, and that I absolutely must not tell my mother of my certain convictions. I have no memory of the rest of that conversation.*
>
> —CLARE, 40

In Clare's case, the shock of knowing that her sibling sixth sense was correct in warning her of her brother's death was almost as shocking as the news itself.

There have been times in my own life when this sibling sixth sense was almost spooky. One particular incident comes immediately to mind. It took place almost twelve years ago, when my younger son, a baby at the time, was very ill. My husband was away on a business trip, and the nearest family member lived three hundred miles away. It was around eleven o'clock at night, long after my bedtime, when I was roused from sleep by a gravelly sounding cough. I stumbled into the nursery and found my baby rolling from side to side, struggling to breathe. I knew that he was having an acute attack of croup (he had had several attacks in the past) and knew exactly what to do, but this was the first time I'd had to handle such an emergency alone. I immediately took the baby into the bathroom and turned the hot shower on full force, filling the room with steam. Somehow I had the presence of mind to bring the phone into the bathroom with me in case things worsened and I needed to call an ambulance.

With two other small children asleep upstairs, I worried about how we would manage if the baby needed to be taken to the hospital. I sat on the bathroom floor, talking softly to my son, praying that this crisis would pass. Just then, the phone rang. The sound startled both the baby and me; we looked at each other and blinked. As I answered the phone, I somehow knew that it was my brother before he even said hello. "Is everything okay?" he asked, concerned. Apparently, he'd been watching television and felt a sudden urgency to call me. Knowing that I usually went to bed early, he had hesitated to call so late. "But," he said, "I had this overwhelming feeling that something was wrong." I'd never been so glad to hear the sound of his voice. We talked for about an hour, until my son's breathing returned to normal. Then I tucked him snugly into his crib.

. . .

There are times, even five years after my brother's death, when I am startled at the realization that he is truly gone, that I will never again hear the sound of his comforting voice, see his face, or feel his familiar bear hug. I sometimes wonder how I was able to move through those early days of grief, when the ponderous weight of his death threatened to crush me.

That first horrible day of grief lasted until well into the night before I finally slept in a world that, for the first time in my life, did not include my brother. But the dreamless sleep lasted only a few hours; I awoke with a start, confused. Something had happened, but what? Then the answer, "Your brother died," came like a slap. This would be the first of many times I would wake and forget for a few moments that he was gone—but this first night was by far the most difficult. I crawled out of bed, pulled the old afghan around my shoulders, and returned to my place on the couch. Less than twenty-four hours had passed since that abysmal phone call; the cordless phone lay uncharged on the floor like a discarded toy. I stared out the window until the cold, gray darkness gave way to the first hint of dawn. I was amazed that the sun should remember to rise amid such sadness.

And then, without warning, the tears came; the sudden rush of choking misery that would visit me often now. Hopelessness, fear, and an agonizing sorrow consumed me, and I was completely lost to it.

Shock grips us, shakes us for a brief time, and then tosses us aside. As the acute feelings of disbelief begin to recede, little by little—like a huge iron door that opens just a crack, allowing a thin sliver of light to cut the darkness—the panic, fear, confusion, and unreality of the situation slowly give way to the dawning sense that this thing, this awful thing, has really happened. The door edged open for me early that morning as the rest of the world blissfully slumbered.

Outside, dogs bark, cars pass, a streetlight turns off, and the faint sound of music is heard in the distance—blasphemies all. You ask yourself, "What do I do now?" and from the jagged shores of shock, a plan slowly begins to take shape. Instinctively, you understand that beyond the door is a new world of uncertainty, suffering, and unimagined sorrow. If the shock you're feeling at this moment is a prelude to what lies ahead, then the only choice is to go back to your life as it was, perhaps just minutes or hours before, when the world was a safe place and your brother or sister was still alive. This plan, so brilliantly simple, first stirs in your subconscious the moment you receive the news that your sibling is gone; you realize that all you need to do is close the door and retreat into the world of denial.

WHAT HELPS

One of the most troubling aspects of grief is the powerlessness associated with it; we know there's nothing that we can do to change the terrible course of events that has invaded our lives. But while it is true that you cannot change the fact that your sibling has passed away, there *are* some things you can do to help yourself navigate the next few days and weeks. (Although you are likely to move in and out of shock for up to a month or longer, the focus here is on short-term, immediate help.)

Without a doubt, the very best thing you can do is to take care of yourself physically. This suggestion may seem self-evident, but remember, you've just been through a terrible trauma; you may be feeling confused, frightened, and exhausted. Even normal activities such as eating and sleeping are often neglected during shock (and early grief), but both are important in helping you to get through the first few days of adjustment to the news that your brother or sister has died. Here are a few helpful suggestions to keep in mind:

- You may have to have someone remind you to eat and drink, because you may not have the body symptoms of hunger and thirst. Lack of food and water will exacerbate many of the physical symptoms of grief, such as light-headedness and stomach upset. Simply remembering to eat can help to control or eliminate such symptoms.

- Light, simple snacks seem to be better than larger meals.
- Carry a water bottle with you to remind you to drink.

Sleeping will probably be difficult during the first few days and weeks after your sibling's death, and you may find that you cannot sleep for more than a few hours at a time. This is a normal grief reaction, but it will rapidly take its toll on your physical and emotional well-being. If possible, try to nap during the day, especially if you find you're not sleeping at all during the night. Lack of sleep will probably intensify most of your feelings and actually make you feel worse. If sleep problems persist for more than a couple of weeks, see your doctor about prescribing a sleeping aid. Be sure to tell your doctor the circumstances of your inability to sleep, as there are some medications that work better than others for the sleeping problems associated with grief.

If you're having trouble sleeping, you should avoid both alcohol and caffeine, especially in the evening. You might even consider avoiding them altogether during this time. Alcohol, in particular, is a depressant, and you're probably more than depressed enough already! Many people self-medicate with alcohol, especially in early grief, and the results are usually disastrous. Alcohol has the effect of temporarily blunting our emotions, but in the end it simply contributes to a deeper depression. Remember: Taking care of yourself is something that is within your power. If you are a person who's not in the habit of taking care of yourself, then the lesson begins now.

Shock has a way of upsetting our internal clocks. Work, meals, sleep, and the normal rhythm of our lives slip into a sort of suspend mode I call *grief time*. Ask people who have experienced intense grief and they will tell you that grief time is a very real phenomenon and differs greatly from real time. You want time to pass quickly because you know that with the passage of time, the sting of grief will be less painful. Unfortunately, at least in the beginning, time moves excruciatingly slowly. Adjusting to grief time is difficult at first, and you will likely find it frustrating, but it is one of many adjustments you will be forced to make during the next few months. Eventually, you'll learn to accept the fact that grief takes time and that it is truly a process that moves at its own pace for each of us.

I experienced shock for the better part of two months, perhaps even longer. I thought I was feeling again after about a month, only to realize I was still in shock. —KATHY B., 37

Perhaps the most important thing to keep in mind through the entire bereavement process is this: You are entitled to feel whatever it is you are feeling. Try not to listen to others who scrutinize your feelings or tell you that you should or should not be feeling a certain way. Feelings are not a choice; they are simply your own response to an event. Typically, surviving siblings in shock aren't quite sure just *what* they are feeling. Soon, however, you are likely to be deluged with a variety of feelings you've never experienced before. Kathy-Anne's advice is profound in its simplicity.

A priest told me, "You will have a whole basket full of emotions. Feel them all. Don't postpone your feelings." That was important advice, but I did not follow it. I'll always remember him saying it, though. —KATHY-ANNE, 53

The first step in your journey, then, is to give yourself permission to *feel*. This may seem deceptively easy; the reality, however, is that we live in a culture that denies death and grief. Although you will likely find an initial outpouring of concern and support that will probably be helpful to you in the short term, know now that this initial support will almost certainly not last beyond a few weeks. Still, as much as possible, try to accept the support offered to you as you move in and out of shock.

With this in mind, another helpful step in your journey is to try to identify at least one person with whom you feel safe and comfortable in sharing your feelings. Within the first week of bereavement, ask this person to be your *grief partner*. A grief partner is a person to whom you can turn, on a daily basis if necessary, to share your feelings. This person need not be an expert in matters of loss and bereavement, but you should be able to trust him or her, and he or she should be compassionate and willing to simply listen. Your grief partner should also be willing and able to help you attend to some of the practical matters associated with losing your sibling, such as dealing with funeral homes and lawyers, and helping you to find time to grieve.

Ideally, this person should also be a surviving sibling, but it can be anyone whom you trust. If you have other brothers and sisters with whom you are close, you might naturally feel that one of them would be an ideal grief partner, since he or she probably understands better than anyone else what you are going through. I would caution against choosing one of your own siblings, as he or she probably won't be in any position to help you. Remember that your siblings, too, will be dealing with their own loss. Many people complain that they feel uncomfortable asking someone to help them. If this applies to you, then I strongly urge you to consider sharing your feelings with a grief therapist. You may lack the emotional energy to go through the process of selecting a grief therapist right now, but I mention it here as an option for you to begin thinking about (see chapter 7 for more information on selecting a grief therapist).

One of the unique features of adult sibling loss is that quite often it's the surviving brother or sister who is responsible for making phone calls to other family members and friends of the deceased, informing them of the terrible news. This is especially true in cases where your sibling is unmarried or your parents are deceased or elderly. It may be difficult for you to carry out this responsibility because you, too, are in shock. Having a support person (grief partner) in place who is there specifically for you offers a much-needed emotional safety net. Although the task of delivering bad news is a difficult one, it may actually have the effect, as in Tracy's case, of helping you to better cope with shock.

> *There were constant phone calls during those first few days, many of which involved breaking the news to family and friends. With each call—every conversation, really—I recited the details of my sister's accident. As I heard the grief and condolence in their voices and with enough repetitions, I began to accept the truth. My sister was really gone.* —TRACY, 41

You have just received terrible news, and you're probably still reeling from the shock of it all. You may be feeling lost and afraid, uncertain and alone. You may have important work to do, such as funeral planning and all of the attendant activity that accompanies the death of a loved one. You may feel as if you need to put your feelings aside and help your parents cope with the loss of their child. Perhaps others have turned to you for guidance and help at a time when you feel unprepared to give it. Whatever your present situation, know that there are several important steps you can take to help yourself during this difficult time. Taking care of yourself, establishing a grief partner with whom you can express you feelings, and simply giving yourself permission to feel are all ways to empower yourself at a time when you are probably feeling helpless and alone.

2

DENIAL

This Can't Be Happening!

At other times, it feels like being mildly drunk, or concussed.
There is a sort of invisible blanket between the world and me.

—C. S. LEWIS

M Y CHILDREN step off the school bus in front of our house and crunch their way up the frozen driveway toward the kitchen door. They move slowly, dragging their backpacks behind them like heavy anchors; even on this cold afternoon, they're in no hurry to get inside. I can't really blame them; grief permeates our house, and silence has replaced the normal busy clamor of family life. Three days have passed since my brother's death and no one, including me, knows how to behave.

I tried to go to work today, but that didn't feel right; I left after a few hours, exhausted and dazed—I can't even remember driving home. I tried cleaning my bedroom, but that didn't feel right, either; I couldn't decide where to begin. I thought about phoning a friend, but who? All of my friends were at work, happily going about their days without a care. Besides, what would I say? "Hello, it's me. I have no idea what to do with myself."

I walk into the family room, turn on the television, and stand in front of it for a few moments. Distracted, I wander into the kitchen, leaving Regis and Kathie Lee to yammer on about the newest spring fashions without me. I go purposely down the stairs into the basement laundry and stand for a long time, trying to remember why I was there in the first place. Then I start to cry. Again.

What am I supposed to do?

I seem to vacillate between numbness and hysteria, bewildered and lost in my own home. I end up spending most of the day just sitting, staring at the wall. Not at a print or a pattern in the wallpaper, just the blank wall. For the first time in my life, my mind is devoid of all thought; there is only a faint hum whirling around the place where my thoughts used to be. The numbness is punctuated every so often by a sudden surge of grief, a spasm really, that strikes without warning, bursting forth from the same blackness that mutes my thoughts.

At my brother's request, there has been no funeral. His ashes remain sequestered a thousand miles away, awaiting the memorial service he asked us hold in the spring. We honor his dying wishes—intended to spare his loved ones further anguish—but in the absence of any ritual to commemorate his passing, I have a hard time believing he's really gone. There remains no tangible evidence of his death; instead, all around me are scraps of his life: on the refrigerator, the off-center photograph of VJay and me, arms around each other, squinting in the brightness of last summer's sun; the framed print of an angel gently guiding two young children over a rickety footbridge, a housewarming gift from my brother two years ago, hangs prophetically at the top of the stairs. The journal he gave me for my birthday, just last month, sits uneasily on my nightstand, its pages blank, the funny card that accompanied the gift still tucked inside—all evidence of his *life*. How can it be possible he died?

My husband left for work early this morning, and I'm relieved not to have his well-intentioned but awkward attempts at comfort. He spent most of the weekend standing in front of me, examining my face for some clue that would tell him what to do next and speaking to me in the voice he usually reserves for sick children. "Can I get you something?" he'd ask. "Water," I'd reply each time. He'd bring me a glass of water and set it beside me, and then I'd forget to drink it.

The children spent the weekend skittering past me and hiding out in their rooms, glad for once when Monday finally came. They left the house ten minutes early to go to their bus stop, a mere fifteen feet from our back door. Now, as they return home, they're filled with foreboding; grief brings uncertainty, the natural nemesis of all children.

I watch from the window as they approach the kitchen door. They stand on the steps for a few moments before coming into the house, talking quietly in a little huddle, breath rising above their heads in a mingled puff. Finally, they slip quietly into the kitchen and look cautiously around. The house smells wonderful, like cinnamon and chocolate. "Hi guys," I say with forced cheer. "I've been baking."

They stand for a moment in their coats and look at me, and then at each other, wondering what brought about this miraculous transformation. My daughter glances over at the door, and I half expect her to run outside to check the number on the house; surely they must have walked into the wrong kitchen. Where is the tearful, inconsolable mother they left this morning? And just who is this dressed up, flour-smudged, June Cleaver impostor greeting them in the kitchen with cookies and muffins?

What my children do not know is this: At some point during the day, between the numbness and the tears, I closed a door. It's almost as if my soul peered warily down the long, dark hallway that lay ahead and decided that it would be better for me not to go there. Heeding the silent warnings from within, I retreated into the world of denial.

Denial, for me, is not a conscious choice, but more of an automatic response. Not yet ready to face the reality of living in a world without my brother, I seek refuge in the familiarity of my kitchen. Standing on a chair and rummaging through cabinets in the same black suit I had worn to work, I feel normal for a while, almost as if grief took a gentlemanly step aside and allowed me this gift. On some level, of course, I know I'm hiding behind the skirts of denial, but I suppress any analysis of my behavior and simply allow myself to be absorbed in the rudimentary tasks of sifting, measuring, and mixing. This temporary escape into my kitchen to bake cookies and muffins is an example of what I call a *diversionary activity*. A diversionary activity, as the name implies, is a brief distraction from the intensity of grief and is a distinctive feature of denial.

Shortly after my brother's death, I cut my long hair and, for the first time in my life, color it. I'm surprised to learn that all three of my sisters and my mother, within weeks of my brother's death, do the same. At first, I think our behavior an odd coincidence or perhaps rooted in some innate, primitive grief response. I know, for example, that in many ancient cultures, cutting off one's hair (or beard) following the death of a loved one was a recognized symbol of mourning. But I now view these actions as diversionary, part of the larger aspect of denial.

Denial provides an escape hatch from grieving, and although the way in which we escape differs, there's no doubt the temporary respite from mourning is, in most cases, beneficial. Perhaps the most common form of escape is a premature return to work. "I need to get back to a regular routine," say bereaved brothers and sisters. Since it's unlikely any person in early grief is very productive, returning to work is probably a diversionary activity, a way of engaging in something familiar and normal when everything else in your life feels alien and abnormal.

One surviving sibling, an avid runner, told me, "I stepped up my running so that I ran five or six miles every day, sometimes twice a day. It was almost as if I was running away from the grief." Whether it's baking, working, or running, diversionary activities offer a welcome break from the intensity of grief.

What got me through the next month after Lori's [age 31] death was taking care of her children and all of the chores that go along with keeping a family and house together. Lori's husband stayed away from the house most of the time, and I did everything. I was so consumed with exhaustion that, for the most part, I felt as if I were just going through the motions. I kept

thinking that I had to keep everything together for Lori's kids,
ages 4, 9, and 11. —DEBBIE, 37

Of course, sometimes, others may misinterpret our behavior. For example, a quick return to work or increased interest in running might be viewed as an uncaring reaction to a sibling's death. Others might conclude that you view the loss of your sibling as insignificant ("She's obviously not taking this loss very hard because she went back to work in less than a week"). Worse, this may contribute to a lack of validation of your grief.

While most surviving siblings report that the initial, sometimes immobilizing shock of grief is often followed by a period of denial or disbelief, just what does it mean to be *in denial*? I always thought of denial as a weakness of character, an indication of some deeper psychological neurosis or, at the very least, something to be avoided. Even the word *denial* has a bad reputation today. Being told you're in denial is almost an epitaph; if you're in denial, then you must be delusional or living in a fantasy world. If you're in denial, then you must need therapy or medication; you certainly can't be normal. While this may be partly true in certain circumstances, I now believe that the feelings of denial associated with the death of a loved one serve an important emotional purpose.

For example, learning your brother or sister has died often conjures frightening and upsetting thoughts and images. Thinking about your brother's or sister's last moments, images of his or her dead body, and many other disturbing mental pictures emerge in your waking thoughts and often disturb your sleep. For obvious reasons, this is an aspect of early grief rarely discussed by surviving siblings.

It was so hard to walk out of the hospital after Bill [age 26]
died. I kept picturing Bill being rushed to the hospital with some
hope of living, and now, his body would be flown to Pittsburgh

for burial. Prior to that, an autopsy would be performed. There were many images flashing through my head, all of them grue-some. The fall weather was so beautiful as we drove from Michigan back to Pennsylvania. The leaves seemed to be bursting with color. The air was crisp and the sun was bright. Yet I felt like I was part of a nightmarish surreal painting. Colors were scream-ing at me in the harsh light. —JULIE, 37

These thoughts and images naturally intensify the shock and pain we're already feeling, and we struggle to rid our minds of such disturbing imaginings, but how? One way is through denial.

"I want it all to go away," I recall telling my husband one evening. "I want to reverse these last few weeks and go back to the way it used to be. I'd do anything just to have this not be true."

My brother Tommy [age 36] died in the attack on the World Trade Center on September 11, 2001. We had such a prolonged period of not knowing. I had a few days of running around with my younger brother, Jimmy, looking in hospitals to see if we could find Tommy—to see if maybe he had gotten out before the tower fell, or even ridden the tower down. (So many of us, including the media, actually believed that was possible! It seems ridiculous to me now!) Because we had those few days of not knowing anything, it made it harder to reconcile myself to the idea that he died when the building collapsed. With all the tele-vision coverage, which we watched religiously that day to find any news of Tommy, I think I was able to deny it was real. Intel-lectually, I knew Tommy was in the building, but on some level, it couldn't be! Tommy couldn't be in that! It must be a horrible movie. It still seems unreal—almost as if I just watch the movie again, there will be a different ending and Tommy won't have been in his office. —KATHY B., 37

Like many surviving siblings, part of my experience of denial is my inability to accept my own helplessness. "There must be something I can do, some deal I can cut, some arrangement I can make," I say quietly, watching from the window as my neighbor unloads groceries from the trunk of her car. My husband looks up from his newspaper and asks cautiously, "Deal? What kind of a deal? What are you talking about?"

"Oh, never mind," I say, amazed I've actually said aloud something I thought I was only thinking.

Although it may seem strange, the truth is, many surviving siblings attempt to bargain with God or make impossible vows to themselves, offering to change their ways or to make atonement for past sins, if only the painful reality swirling about them could be reversed. While Elisabeth Kübler-Ross and others understood bargaining as part of the greater spectrum of shock (especially with regard to dying patients), bargaining seems to be especially connected to denial, as in Victoria's case.

> *Every day, for weeks, I prayed to God to allow Susan [age 17] to return to us. "God, I won't let anyone know if you give us this miracle. Susan and I can live together in another state. Please, God, let her come back to us so we can do things differently. Don't allow our lives to be forever ruined!" Somehow, I really believed that God would be able to breathe life into Susan's dead body and allow her to emerge from her buried casket. I had a lot of irrational thoughts.* —VICTORIA, 26

As Victoria observes, in retrospect, bargaining may seem irrational; but in early grief, most of us stumble through the process, feeling powerless and lost, searching for a lifeline, a way to escape the reality of the situation. What is the lifeline that enables us to hold on during a time when letting go seems preferable? *Denial.*

Actually, living in a temporary state of denial allows us to function in what appears to be a normal fashion. Despite the fact we've just lost a sibling, we somehow summon the strength to attend to the morbid end-of-life details that are often the responsibility of surviving siblings. Have you ever noticed the remarkable ability of mourners to greet those gathered to pay their last respects to the deceased with appropriate social grace? Bereaved persons are able to carry on intelligent conversations, sometimes even laughing and joking with family and friends. They appear normal during a time of extreme duress.

Others may even comment, when asked how the family is holding up under such difficult circumstances, that the family appears to be doing quite well. How can this be? What is it that enables us to find the strength at precisely the time when we would have expected our resources to be virtually depleted? *Denial.* How else can we explain the sister who is able to make plane reservations, pack, and travel to her brother's funeral when she has learned, only hours before, that he was murdered? What enables the brother to stand beside the casket of his dead sister and shake the hands of mourners as they pass by in a receiving line? *Denial.*

In most cases, experiencing denial is not something terrible or pathological. Being in denial does not mean that you are weak or crazy or helpless. On the contrary, denial is the way in which our wonderful minds move forward to buffer the terrible impact of our brother's or sister's death. It appears in full force when we need it the most, softening the blow of grief.

> *For months, whenever I thought of Stefani's [age 25] death, I would get to the point where in my mind I would scream, "No! This is too terrible to be true!" I've always thought of denial as something unhealthy and negative. Looking back, however, I think my denial was a means for me to gradually and more gently move toward a manageable level of acceptance.*
>
> —DEAN, 30

When I think of denial, I am reminded of something psychiatrists call the *delusion of reprieve*. The delusion of reprieve occurs when the condemned person, just prior to his execution, maintains the illusion that his sentence will be commuted at the last moment—that he will live, not die. This delusion is in keeping with the human inability to truly envision our own death.

Denial, or delusion of reprieve, when understood as a sort of psychological protective mechanism, accounts for the hope expressed by many siblings that things might not be as bad as they seem. Surviving sibling Carolyn expresses such hope after receiving the news that two of her brothers had been involved in a fatal accident.

> *It was a beautiful day when I lost two of my four younger brothers, Dougie [age 26] and Denny [age 23]. I waved to them as they left to go hunting. I can still see Denny's wonderful smile as he waved back to me. Late that night, my brother Kevin broke the news that Denny was dead and that Dougie was in the intensive care unit. The ride to the hospital with my folks was a nightmare—all sorts of excuses about how it could not be my brothers who had been in the accident. Perhaps someone had stolen their wallets, or the police had made a mistake. Maybe this was just a nightmare that I was having, and I would wake up and find that they were both safe, at home.* —CAROLYN, 48

As we try to come to terms with the shocking news of a brother or sister's death, we reasonably conjecture that perhaps there has been some hideous mistake. Like Carolyn (and Rosemary, below) we might, for example, convince ourselves that there has been a simple case of mistaken identity. (After all, most of us have read stories of such things happening.) Our minds scramble to protect us from the trauma of such a horrible reality as a frantic voice, deep within us, cries out against the injustice of the situation. "This cannot be happening!" we protest. "Not to my sibling! Not to my family!"

> *I was sure that the army had somehow mixed up the bodies or that someone else was probably using Sean's [army officer] pass to get into the squash club [where Sean suffered a fatal heart attack at age 43], and we would all find out that there was some mistake. When I saw the look on my parents' faces the next day at the airport, I knew there was no mistake.*
>
> —ROSEMARY, 51

• • •

Like so many other families today, my siblings and I grew up and moved away from our hometown; we're scattered along the East Coast and see each other only a few times a year. My brother lived in Florida and I live in Rhode Island, so we became experts in the art of maintaining a relationship through phone calls and letters. But because we lived so far apart, after his death it was easy for me to pretend he was still alive. At first, there were times when I simply forgot he was gone. I'd go to the phone to share a story or problem with him, and then a squeeze of shock, suddenly fresh and painful all over again, would remind me he wasn't here anymore.

Over time, denial seems to move from an instinctual, unconscious response to a sort of conscious coping tool. On a very real level, I know my brother is gone, but because we lived in different states, it's sometimes easier for me to imagine he's still alive and well, sunning himself on the patio of his condo or walking on the beach, collecting shells. When I talk about this with my younger sister, Tracy, who has become my daily sounding board for sanity, she sighs with relief.

"I thought I was the only one sometimes pretending he was still alive," she confesses, and then admits, "I even called his house a couple of times just to listen to his voice on the recorder before it was disconnected."

I used denial a lot during the first year or two. Although I knew that Danny [age 23] was really dead, I used to pretend that he was just away, on one of his trips. —LINDA-LEE, 49

I occasionally indulged myself by thinking that maybe Stefani really didn't die. Maybe it was someone else who only looked like her. Maybe Stefani was really alive and well somewhere. Of course, I knew that couldn't be the case, but losing Stefani was so tragic that I allowed myself to ponder the possibility that I wouldn't have to live the rest of my life without seeing her again, that there had to be some sort of freak mix-up. I engaged in this type of denial periodically for several months after Stefani's death. Even now, four years later, on rare occasions, I still think about how wonderful it would be if there had *been a mix-up and Stefani was alive somewhere.* —DEAN, 30

But how long does denial generally last? How long is too long? For me, the acute phase of denial is relatively short lived, but like Linda-Lee and Dean, denial actually helps me to little by little accept my brother's death; I return to it many times during those first difficult weeks, or rather, it returns to me. So the best response to the question "How long?" with regard to any aspect of grief, including denial, is "As long as it takes." Despite social convention and advice from the experts, there's really nothing wrong with taking the time necessary to find your own way through grief. So what if it takes you a little longer for the reality of your sibling's death to sink in? You may need that additional time to process what has happened.

Ongoing denial, whereby one refuses to accept the reality of a sibling's death to the point of denying the loss has even taken place, can, however, be serious. It is possible to become stuck in grief at any phase of your journey, and you should be aware of this possibility. In such cases, it is prudent to consider talking to a competent therapist who is well versed in grief-related issues. Fortunately, this type of denial is rare.

• • •

A few weeks after my brother's death, an old friend, Butler, phones to offer his condolences. My husband calls me to the phone and away from the stack of papers I've been grading. As I cross the room to take the phone, I'm ambushed; I'm suddenly overcome by a spasm of grief so intense I find it difficult to breathe, much less carry on a conversation. I try to compose myself enough to speak to my friend, but I end up handing the phone back to my husband and leaving the room.

I feel ashamed and humiliated, weak and helpless. "Butler must think I'm crazy," I mutter to myself as I splash cool water on my face. I spend the rest of the evening sitting alone in my bedroom, trying to understand what had happened. I thought I'd been dealing with my loss well and believed things were actually getting better. I was writing about my feelings in my grief journal and sharing my thoughts with a few trusted friends and family members. Why the sudden attack of grief? What precipitated this? How could such intense emotions surface without warning? How long would this last?

After that day, the grief intensifies instead of getting better. (So much for the promises of those who tell me "with time comes healing," I think bitterly.) I begin crying more and have problems concentrating and sleeping. When I do sleep, I'm plagued with disturbing dreams that make little sense—at least, the parts I can remember. I have one particularly bizarre dream in which I'm slipping and sliding backward on a muddy slope. A thunderous rain makes it impossible for me to see as I grope blindly in the darkness for something to steady my wobbly descent to the bottom of the hill. In the dream, I know something terrifying awaits me at the bottom of the hill. When I write about this dream in my grief journal, I interpret the dream positively as a symbol of my underlying strength in dealing with my loss. I now wonder, however, if the dream signaled instead my desire to cling to the safety of denial. To remain on the slippery hill, precarious as it was, sure beat the alternative of tumbling headlong into the unknown abyss below.

I tell my sister Tracy about the grief getting worse instead of better, and she replies, "I know. It's been getting worse for me, too." None of this makes any sense. "I don't understand," I tell her, genuinely confused. "Up until a few days ago, I felt as if things were improving. Now I feel as if I'm sliding backward," I say, the disturbing mudslide dream still fresh in my thoughts.

We ponder this truth for a moment, and then Tracy ventures, "Maybe we're just starting to *really* believe he's gone and that he's *really* not coming back—that this is final." I start to correct her, to tell her I know our brother is gone and I painfully feel his absence every moment of every day—but then I understand her meaning. Even though I'd been telling myself things were getting better, in reality, things weren't getting better at all; I'd simply ducked behind the fence of denial.

I hang up the phone and go for a long walk, forgetting my mittens. I stick my fists deep into my pockets and draw my collar up around my neck. White clouds hurry past overhead and a chilly wind gathers leaves in a circle before blowing them into the gutter. I walk faster, trying to keep warm as I fend off disturbing thoughts and images of my brother's last days. I feel the security of denial slowly melting away, withdrawing its protective hand and pointing me in the direction of the dark hallway I've been avoiding.

Several days later, I open the door and start down that dreaded dark hallway, alone and without a flashlight.

WHAT HELPS

From a distance, you're aware of others moving about, talking, consoling. There's a flurry of activity and muted voices, but it all seems so far away. Nothing seems real; it must be a dream or a movie, or perhaps this is all happening to someone else and you're just a detached observer. Your mind feels thick, like pudding. You're confused and anxious, but most of all, you just want it all to go away. If this description captures some of the emotions you're presently feeling, then you're probably experiencing some form of denial.

So what helps during this difficult time of disbelief?

First, continue to be proactive about taking care of yourself. Try to eat several small meals a day (though you probably won't have much of an appetite), get plenty of rest (though you'll probably have trouble sleeping), keep hydrated, and avoid alcohol and caffeine. Beyond that, the advice is fairly simple: Accept denial as part of the way you're processing your grief. This sounds simple, of course, but it's actually pretty difficult for most grieving people to accept their feelings, especially when it comes to denial. After all, you've probably already received subtle (and overt) messages from others, dictating how you *should* behave.

Shakespeare wrote, "That that is is." As I've already stressed, denial isn't good or bad or anything else. It just is.

Having said this, I think it's important to stress once again the ways in which people's grief can differ. While some surviving siblings may be obvious in their bereavement, others may appear more circumspect and quiet. Even if there seem to be no outward signs of grief, that doesn't mean the person isn't mourning. It's been pretty standard fare among most grief experts to assert that if a person doesn't cry and openly express his or her sorrow, the repressed grief will eventually surface in other unhealthy ways. This may be true for some, but not for all. I've spoken to many surviving siblings who both love and miss their deceased brothers and sisters but who also report an absence of what most of us consider typical grief behaviors, such as crying and depression. It's entirely possible, then, to misinterpret certain grieving differences as denial when, in fact, what is being experienced is not denial at all.

Next, realize that although denial may actually help carry you through those first terrible days and weeks, the anesthetic will eventually wear off. This may happen all at once, or little by little. There were times, shortly after my brother's death, when I would think to myself, "This really isn't so bad. I can do this." It wasn't long, however, before the false sense of bravado dissolved into a fear so intense that my insides actually shivered.

The factors discussed in chapter 1—whether your sibling's death was expected or sudden, the amount of support you receive, your particular personality—all can contribute to the manner in which you experience (or don't experience) denial. For example, if your sibling's death was anticipated, then you are less likely to remain in denial about it for very long. Of course, this may not always be the case, but a sudden death generally results in more prolonged and intense feelings of denial.

Finally, be warned: As a surviving sibling, you may be expected to take care of certain tasks during a time when you'd just as soon stick your head in the sand. If your parents are still alive, they're likely to lean on their other surviving children to help them take care of your sibling's end-of-life details, such as emptying your brother's or sister's house and planning the funeral. If your parents are deceased and your sibling was not married or partnered, then you, like Sunny, may be the only person available to make such arrangements.

After Bob [age 48] died, I was completely alone in a city where I knew nobody. The few people who had been at his bedside had

all gone their separate ways, but I had to stay behind and make
the arrangements. It was terrible. I have never in my life felt so
completely desolate. I picked up the phone and called faraway
friends and relatives, but no one seemed to understand, which
made me feel worse. —SUNNY, 75

Because you've just experienced a trauma yourself, you probably lack both the physical and emotional energy right now to make any major decisions. In fact, most psychologists advise against making any important, irreversible decisions during bereavement, especially when your judgment is clouded by denial. (Now is not the time, for example, to purchase a new home or change jobs.) Unfortunately, your parents (and others) may rely on you to take charge. This means you'll probably be required to make certain decisions concerning the disposition of your brother's or sister's personal effects, as well as helping to arrange his or her funeral. You may wonder how anyone could possibly lean on you right now, when you can't even think clearly enough to decide what shoes to wear.

Before we discuss the two tasks, emptying your sibling's home and planning his or her funeral (the two most common duties expected of surviving siblings), let's first review a few general guidelines that will help you deal better with denial. First, even though you're struggling with your own anguish over losing your sibling, there are certain obligations that just don't go away. For example, if you have a family of your own, you must continue to care for them; if you have a job, you'll need to arrange time off. And other duties and responsibilities outside home and work will need to be suspended for a period of time. Of course, all of this requires phone calls and schedule juggling. Because you're likely to feel anxious, befuddled, and not completely in control right now, every chore, every request, every obligation probably seems like an insurmountable task.

Since you're not thinking clearly, it's wise to get into the habit of writing things down. Carry a small notebook around with you to record names, numbers, dates, and other important reminders to help keep you focused. While you're in this state of mind, keep a satchel or a backpack with you at all times stocked with the following items: a water bottle, aspirin, your notebook, pens, a few snacks, your cell phone, and lots of tissues.

You'll also need a clearheaded person to help you make decisions; this person, ideally, should be your grief partner. Try to involve your grief partner as much as possible. Beyond providing emotional support, he or she can offer practical advice and help you wade through the confusing paperwork and numerous details that may seem crushing to you right now. Bring your grief partner to meetings with funeral directors, clergy, florists, and attorneys.

Be sure to take notes at these meetings, and ask your grief partner to take notes as well. Make certain all procedures, dates, and documents are carefully explained to you. Of course, don't sign anything unless you understand what you're signing. Although much of this sounds like common sense, in your present state of mind, meetings, legal forms, and nearly everything else may seem fairly meaningless and unimportant compared to what you've lost. In the greater scheme of things, you're probably right. Nonetheless, you still want and need to do the right thing—for the rest of your family and yourself, and to honor your sibling's memory.

Whenever possible, have your grief partner make phone calls, arrange meetings, and cancel obligations; ask others to phone you to remind you of important dates. But most of all, be honest with people and tell them, "I've just lost my sibling, so I'm not really myself right now." Most people will be understanding and accommodating.

. . .

If you find yourself assigned the unhappy task of emptying your brother's or sister's home, you need to prepare yourself for a flood of conflicting feelings. If it's at all possible, you might want to delay this sad chore for several weeks. Unfortunately, if your brother or sister lived in a rental property, the landlord will most likely require this to be done sooner rather than later.

Sorting through the paperwork, clothing, treasures, and other personal articles that helped define who your sibling was in this life is probably one of the most emotionally challenging tasks survivors will have to do. There's something intimate and sacred about a person's living space, and you may feel like an intruder as you riffle through your sibling's private world. If you're in denial when you begin this sad and difficult task, you won't be when you're through. Packing up your sibling's clothing, reading his or her mail, disconnecting the answering machine and telephone, even emptying the medicine cabinet are all clear and irrefutable evidence of his or her demise. If you have other surviving siblings who are able and willing to help you, try to do this together.

> *Dealing with my own feelings, thoughts, and emotions was hard after my brother's death, but the hardest part was seeing my parents in so much pain. They have always been my rock throughout my life, and the one time that they both needed to lean on me, I couldn't do a very good job. Thank goodness for my older brother and sister. Between all of us, we have pulled together and survived.* —TAMI, 26

At the very least, enlist the support of your grief partner or close friends. Having someone along for emotional support and to help you sort, box, donate, or dispose of your sibling's belongings can be a great comfort, especially if you, like Janet, happen to stumble upon something hurtful or critical of you as a sibling.

> *Having moved into my brother's house, I have had much sorting and decision making to do. Among his papers, I found old jour-*

nals and diaries, most of which were in reference to his very painful divorce that took place in the 1980s. He had gone into therapy soon thereafter and had done some very serious soul-searching. I was shocked and disappointed to see my name mentioned here and there, mostly in unflattering terms. It seems that in his mind, I had never been the sister he needed me to be, that I had always fallen short. He had a similar attitude toward the rest of the family. I read these things thoroughly, felt very bad, and then recalled my own attitude back in the 1980s as actually very similar. At this point, ten years later, I believe (I WANT to believe) that we both grew beyond that negativity and reached a point where we accepted our bond, forgave each other, and chose to allow our siblinghood to develop in healthy and rewarding ways. It is very important for me to think that at the time of Jim's death, we were on loving terms and had left no serious loose ends dangling. —JANET, 57

In addition to emptying your sibling's home, you'll probably be involved, at least to some degree, in planning the funeral. Even if you have other siblings around to help with the funeral arrangements, you might consider including your grief partner as a support person just for you. Although planning a funeral may seem like an overwhelming responsibility, especially when you're knee deep in denial, remember, you're not alone in the process. In addition to your grief partner, there are caring professionals who will help you to personalize your sibling's memorial service or funeral, but you'll need to be specific. Funeral directors, for example, can be extremely helpful in making the necessary arrangements, including obituaries, interment, and expected social conventions associated with funerals. My advice here is to seek their professional guidance as much as possible.

The same is true of clergy. Most are caring and compassionate, and they want the service to be meaningful to you and your family. Funerals offer a unique opportunity for you (and others) to express your feelings of love, gratitude, and loss. Special music, people, and rituals that help commemorate your sibling's life should serve as the backbone of the service. You might also consider speaking at the funeral or memorial service. You may simply choose to tell a story about your brother or sister that illustrates what kind of person he or she was, or you may decide to honor your sibling in song, poetry, or prayer. Speaking from the heart, as someone who knew your sibling for a lifetime, is perhaps the most moving tribute. If you have other surviving siblings, you might work together to present a eulogy. One surviving sibling, from a large, musical family, told me about a musical montage she and her other siblings created that embraced their deceased sister's zest for life. "We stood there together and sang our hearts out," she told me. "It was our own special way to celebrate our sister's life."

Although planning a funeral will be difficult for you emotionally, you may find, like Helen, that participating in this process is immensely healing.

What helped the most during phase one was being able to take control of several tasks after JoAnn's [age 54] death (memorial arrangements, meeting with the priest, calling friends and family), which at least made me feel like I was doing something for her, in her memory, and for her loved ones (her husband, her children, and friends). Two things I'm most proud of were writing JoAnn's death notice for the local paper and designing the program that was distributed at her memorial service. Every word in that death notice was chosen with love and respect. I wanted to incorporate elements of God, love, beauty, music, and joy at her memorial service, which (I'm hoping) I was able to accomplish. I think she would have been proud of me.

—HELEN, 46

For Helen, involving herself in JoAnn's memorial service was hugely comforting. This is one of the many reasons why funerals and memorial services are so important. But beyond the comfort they provide, funerals and memorial services often cut through the haze of denial; as a result, you may, for the first time, accept your loss as real. In other words, seeing your sibling's body and the mourners gathered to pay their last respects may result in either a gradual or sudden dissipation of denial.

> *Initially, I decided not to attend Susan's [age 17] rosary service because I knew I would have to see her body and accept the fact that she was really dead. But my father insisted that the whole family attend. As I walked down the aisle toward Susan's casket, supported by my father and brother, I felt a rush of warm feelings. Suddenly, I was filled with the knowledge that Susan was okay and that she was with God. This wonderful, spiritual experience gave me the courage and strength to survive this tragedy.*
>
> —VICTORIA, 26

• • •

Prayer services, memorial services, and funerals symbolize the painful separation we feel from our loved ones. But while such services can be immensely helpful in bereavement, they can also lead people to forget that grief lasts beyond the three days usually allotted to mourning.

In the past, communities relied on established rituals and external symbols of mourning to help gently guide the bereaved through the grief process. Of course, until Kübler-Ross's work on death and dying, people did not talk about grief as a process, nor did they discuss stages of grief. Nevertheless, they understood this simple truth: Grief takes time. Family and friends gathered around the bereaved and helped them to learn to live in a world without their loved one. The bereaved felt comforted by familiar rituals and symbols of mourning that silently spoke to them and whispered, "You're not alone."

Today, in America, most of these rituals and external symbols, such as the wearing of dark clothing, have been abandoned. Mourners often feel displaced in our fast-paced, get-over-it society. This is especially true of surviving siblings, and all other disenfranchised grievers. When those around you either fail to acknowledge your loss, minimize it, or even ignore it, it stands to reason you might have a difficult time believing it, too.

With this in mind, in addition to religious rituals, I propose the reinstitution of several other external symbols of mourning. I believe most people do try to be helpful and caring when they know we are hurting. And external signs or symbols provide just the right kind of gentle reminder. Not only do the following suggestions accommodate grieving differences, they also help ease us out of denial so that we can move forward, at our own measured pace.

My mother tells me that when she was a little girl growing up in Baltimore, external symbols of grief were commonplace. For example, when someone died in the neighborhood, the family of the deceased would hang a wreath with colored ribbons on the door. The color of the ribbons indicated the general age of the person: light purple for an elderly person, yellow for a young person, and white for a child. Other mourners might drape the doorframe in a black bunting.

People understood and respected such external signs and responded with condolences, food gifts, flowers, and words of comfort. Even passersby and strangers recognized the external symbols of mourning and sent prayers to the grieving family within. The wreath and the black bunting, then, became powerful symbols of grief, external signs that asked for the community's understanding, support, and compassion. Brought back, these customs would not only inform the neighborhood and community of a death, they would also symbolize the family's official period of mourning.

Another age-old external sign of grieving is wearing black. In visiting other countries, particularly Italy and Greece, I've often observed those in mourning wearing black or other dark colors. I was told that during the first year after the death of a loved one, it's customary to wear black or dark colors and to avoid festive events, such as weddings or birthday parties. In many cases, European widows continue to wear black for their rest of their lives. Here in the United States, wearing dark colors during bereavement was a pervasive practice until about the early 1950s. I believe this custom should be resurrected.

In the case of sibling loss, wearing black or other dark colors for six weeks seems reasonable, but ultimately only you can decide the length of time you feel comfortable wearing mourning clothes. I wore black for about two months after my brother's death, and though most people seemed not to notice, the dark clothing helped me to feel as if I had honored his memory. I felt as if I was able to reclaim some minuscule amount of power by wearing black and decided that if this made me feel even a tiny bit better, then it was well worth it. In addition to—or in lieu of—wearing mourning clothes, you might decide to wear a black armband or a mourning pin (a small button covered in black satin). Both are available through some funeral homes.

Finally, something that can help you cope better with the feelings associated with denial is to begin keeping a grief journal. I've never been a big journal keeper myself, having failed at every attempt to write beyond a few weeks, but I *did* keep a grief journal. For me, my grief journal provided a much-needed outlet for thoughts and feelings I simply couldn't share with anyone else. I began writing in the journal my brother had given me for my birthday—a sad irony, to be sure, but I felt strangely comforted in using it. I tried not to pay attention to spelling, grammar, and style, but instead wrote whatever came to mind. Many of my early entries were simply strings of words describing my feelings at that particular moment. One typical entry reads, "Tired, numb, scared, my head hurts."

Eventually, I began to elaborate more. "I'm alone in this," I wrote ten days after my brother's death. "I play stupid mind games with myself, pretending that he's still alive, all the while knowing that he's dead. How can the mind believe two such divergent truths?"

If you're like most grieving siblings, summoning the energy to go out and buy a grief journal, much less write in one, may require too much effort—but if you can possibly muster the energy to do this, I think you'll find this small step toward healing quite helpful. Some siblings prefer to purchase a journal with a fancy cover, adorned with angels, flowers, or other comforting images; others choose to decorate their grief journal with photographs of their sibling. A simple spiral-bound notebook works just as well. If your handwriting is as bad as mine, you might even consider keeping a computer journal.

If the idea of a grief journal doesn't appeal to you, you might consider a family journal instead. A family journal is a sort of communal diary. Family members can record their thoughts and feelings and read and respond to the entries written by others. The best way to begin a family journal is to start one yourself. Write in it for a few days and then pass it on to another family member. Eventually, it should be passed back to you in round-robin fashion, with each person writing in it over a period of several days. Families can elect to set specific time periods for each member to have the journal, or settle on a more relaxed method for sharing. Do whatever seems best for your particular family.

If you're living at home with your parents, or if you're married or partnered, you might consider beginning a family journal by simply leaving it out on the kitchen counter for others to read and add their own entries. Family journals can be particularly helpful to families in which talking about feelings is either difficult or not an active part of the family dynamic. A family journal doesn't require all family members to participate; indeed, not everyone may feel they can benefit from such an activity. And other family members should accept an individual's decision not to participate; such acceptance sets the tone of tolerance for different ways of mourning, which, of course, benefits all family members.

The grief journal, whether individual, communal, or both, can be a valuable tool in helping you to express and eventually understand your feelings. Moreover, it may even alert you to possible problems—such as depression—in yourself and in others. Finally, think of your journal as a chronicle of your journey. In a very real sense, it is part of the larger story of you and your sibling.

Accepting your feelings of denial, enlisting support from your grief partner, attending to your brother's or sister's end-of-life details, displaying some external symbol of mourning, and journal writing can be helpful in dealing with early grief, especially denial.

Soon, however, as the protective wall of denial begins to crumble, you're likely to feel exposed, vulnerable, and, sadly, at the mercy of others.

The denial stage is not totally gone. I still think that I will wake up and Sarah [age 36] will be back with us.

—LAURA, 39

3

THE REACTIONS
OF OTHERS

Why Can't You Understand?

*While grief is fresh, every attempt to divert it
only irritates.*

—SAMUEL JOHNSON

HAVING OBSERVED that time-honored New England tradition of rushing to the grocery store to buy bread and milk whenever the threat of snow is in the forecast, I find myself stranded in an interminable line, holding fast to my uncanny ability (which I'm convinced is genetic) to select the slowest cashier in the store. It's the first time I've been in a grocery store since my brother's death three weeks ago. I feel strangely out of place in a store I've patronized weekly for more than ten years. Although the store hasn't changed at all during my three-week hiatus, it *feels* different, in much the same way home feels different after I return from vacation. My mother calls this odd sensation the "stranger in my own house syndrome," and I smile slightly when I think of her apt nomenclature.

I shift the jug of milk to my other hand, regretting my decision not to use a cart. Thoughts of my husband sitting comfortably at home in front of the evening news make me envious and a little angry. "Why didn't he offer to do this?" I wonder. He smiled encouragingly as I put on my coat and gathered my purse and keys. He seemed almost proud to see me head off into the night, as if I had finally overcome some sort of agoraphobic episode. I find his behavior irritating, but I'm not sure why.

As I mull this over, I'm struck by the fact that my husband hasn't even mentioned my brother's death in several days. I quickly conclude that he's probably just tired of it all—sick of my long face, the tears, and the whole grief business. I know none of this is true, but just thinking about it triggers a kind of affronted stab of sadness and anger; and then, I realize, much to my horror, I'm about to cry.

I'm certain all the shoppers have turned to stare at me, their brows narrowed in annoyance. "What's wrong with that woman over there?" they ask one another, shaking their heads in disbelief. I feign a cough, a lame effort to camouflage as a cold the tears brimming in my eyes and the blotchy red streaks now blooming across my cheeks (my stigmata since childhood of impending tears). I'm mortified at the thought of crying while standing in line at the grocery store. "As if losing my brother isn't terrible enough," I lament silently, "now I have to deal with public humiliation."

I look around at the faces of the other shoppers, trying desperately to channel my thoughts in another direction. "Calm down," I tell myself. "Think of something else." I swallow hard and take several deep breaths, certain the bookish couple behind me thinks I'm in the middle of a panic attack. I try to reassure myself: "No one is paying attention; no one knows. I look like a normal person, out buying bread and milk."

After a few moments, I'm thankful to feel the wave retreat. Feeling calmer, I realize this is the first time I've been in a place where "no one knows" since my brother's death. No wonder I'm so on edge. I've moved in the small circle of home and work during the past three weeks, safe in my own little world where everyone "knows."

I take a second look around and wonder whether there are others, standing in line or moving up and down the aisles, who are just like me: broken and grieving, yet pasted together enough to buy milk and bread and worry about snowstorms that may never come. I wonder how it is you can feel so terrible inside, yet appear normal on the outside. For all I know, the store might be filled with grieving people; unlike physical disabilities, the casual observer rarely discerns grief. I ponder this little epiphany, as if I'm the first grieving person ever to stumble upon it. Then, from a distance, I hear someone calling my name.

I follow the voice to an acquaintance, Mary Beth, the quintessential neighborhood busybody, wheeling her carriage in my direction. "Oh no," I think to myself, "I haven't seen her since . . ." (Every event of my life is now categorized in a "before-my-brother-died" or "after-my-brother-died" time frame.) I'm trapped, hemmed in by the new mother in front of me who's buying every box of Pampers on the shelf and the bookish couple behind me. I don't want to talk to anyone, especially someone like Mary Beth, but there's no escape. Besides, I look like a train wreck: windblown hair, eyes ringed in dark, puffy circles, lips dry and chapped. I haven't slept in three weeks, and I've lost ten pounds. "Grief makes you ugly," I told my reflection earlier in the day.

Mary Beth approaches, smiling as if she's just heard something mildly amusing, and parks her carriage beside me. She reaches out and squeezes my forearm with her gloved hand. "Well, where have *you* been?" she asks, as if I've been avoiding her on purpose.

"I've been in hell," I think to myself.

"I haven't seen you since the summer!" she says in a way that makes me feel strangely guilty. "Shopping before the storm?" she chuckles.

I start to reply, but she charges on, eyeing the couple behind me. "So, how have you been? How's Rob and the kids?" I hesitate for a moment; what do I say? Should I pretend nothing's happened? Should tell her about my brother? Sensing my hesitancy, she leans in closer.

"Is something wrong? Are you okay?" she asks without sincerity as she looks around to see if there's anyone else in the store of a higher social status with whom she might have a more fruitful conversation.

Against the urgings of the Voice Within (the intuitive little voice that's guided me through these last weeks), I decide to tell her about my brother's death. The words tumble out, almost as if some unknown force has sucked the words right from my thoughts.

"Actually, Mary Beth, I'm not doing very well." The Voice whispers, "Don't do it! Don't tell her!"

She stiffens and makes eye contact with me for the first time. Now she's interested.

"My brother passed away three weeks ago," I say quietly. Instantly, I wish I could swipe the words from the air before they reach Mary Beth's ears. A pang of regret gathers in my stomach and the Voice rebukes me: "You idiot!"

Why did I tell this woman something so personal and intimate? Am I that desperate for sympathy?

Mary Beth takes a small step backward, her mouth a thin line. She looks at me as if I've ruined a perfectly fine little repartee with my sad news. Then, remembering her manners, she asks a few perfunctory questions in her pleasant telephone voice: "How old was he?" "How are your parents?" "Were you close?" I respond with equally perfunctory answers: "Forty-three." "Terrible." "Yes." Having done her duty, she draws a deep breath and sighs. There's an awkward pause, and then, resuming her chatty voice, she asks, "So, what else is going on?"

I'll never forget that excruciating conversation in the grocery store on that snowy night because I learned two painful but valuable lessons. First, don't expect others to understand the depth of your loss, especially those who are either incapable or unwilling to offer you comfort. Remember, there are many people who do not consider the death of an adult sibling to be a major loss, and so their reaction naturally reflects this viewpoint. Second, when it comes to grief, heed the warnings of the Voice Within. This voice, when acknowledged, can become a helpful guide through the confusing maze of emotions you've probably never felt before. Throughout this book, I stress the importance of tossing away the timetables and rejecting the so-called norms for conventional grief behavior in favor of doing what comes naturally *to you*. Failure to heed this voice, to behave in a way that seems unnatural to you, only complicates grieving.

Looking back on those early weeks following my brother's death, I have often thought of my reactions in certain situations as abnormal, or, at the very least, uncharacteristically odd. For example, anyone who knows me realizes that I'm not a person who cries very easily. I'm usually fairly gregarious and comfortable in most social situations. The tearful recluse spawned by grief was some sort of hybrid version of me, a stranger in many ways even to myself.

> *I wanted to howl and scream and I wanted to do it for a long time (too long?), but I never gave myself the opportunity. I just drank too much and was very irritable. I sometimes think if I had really howled and screamed, I could have been done with it. Instead, I held everything in and tried to be business and life as usual. Things would build up and I would have these really inappropriate, fast outbursts over trivial, silly things, like not being able to find a shoe or having my car not start.*
>
> —FRANCESCA, 43

Many surviving siblings relate similar feelings of odd or abnormal behavior, especially during early bereavement. I'm reminded of something Viktor Frankl (*Man's Search for Meaning*) said about abnormal reactions: "An abnormal reaction in an abnormal situation is normal." Grief is an abnormal situation; thankfully, we don't lose loved ones very often, and so behaving out of character seems normal in the context of grief. In the supermarket story, that strange, out-of-place feeling, the sudden rush of sadness, and my blurting out information I would not normally share with people like Mary Beth are all abnormal reactions for me. In the context of grief, however, those are normal reactions.

Of course, if I had only listened to the Voice Within, I probably wouldn't have even ventured out to a crowded grocery store on the eve of a snowstorm just three weeks after my brother's death, where I was certain to bump into friends and neighbors who might logically ask how I was doing.

But the bigger question remains: Why was Mary Beth's reaction to my loss hurtful enough for me to remember after nearly five years? Moreover, why should any of us care about someone else's reaction to our loss? The reason is that human beings are communal by nature—we live and work, love and grieve, within the context of a larger community—so what others think, do, and say affects us. As much as we might like to believe the reactions of others are unimportant, the truth is that how other people react to our loss *does* matter. Inappropriate, unsupportive, diminishing responses, like Mary Beth's, send a clear and hurtful message: "Your sibling's death is no big deal." Loving, sympathetic, and comforting reactions, on the other hand, validate our feelings and foster healing. Some, like Clare, are fortunate to be surrounded by sympathetic and supportive family and friends.

> *My friends closed in around me, humming with quiet sympathy and distress. That they did not know what to say did not matter; they created a sort of psychological/emotional cast of absolute support and affection that held me together through the long hurting, healing process in the same way a cast holds a broken bone together so that it will knit properly. Moreover, at no time did they give me that garbage about loss being good for your character or making you stronger. They kept my life going for me when I couldn't. I do not know how I would have managed without them.* —CLARE, 40

But, more often than not, surviving siblings often feel the opposite: that their grief is rarely affirmed and generally misunderstood. Still, we expect close friends and family members to rush to our side and walk us through the darkness. But are we expecting too much?

Today, when I talk to my husband about those early weeks and months following my brother's death, he confesses an almost total lack of understanding of the depth of my loss. If my husband, who is closest to me, failed to understand my grief, it's little wonder others also failed.

> *My husband did some harm since he thought that talking about Jeanne's [age 47] death all of the time would just make me feel worse. Yet what I most needed to do was to talk about every aspect of the eight weeks I spent with her while she was dying.*
>
> —NANCI, 60

> *My brother, Scott [age 23], was murdered—shot in the face in a bar. My then husband refused to even discuss it; he acted like it never happened.* —KATHRYN, 42

There is often a strange paradox associated with the loss of a sibling: For many of us, the person to whom we normally turn for love and support in times of crisis has been our deceased brother or sister. This was certainly true in my case; it was my big brother who acted as the calming presence in my life, the wise voice of reason who helped me make sense out of the confusing and often tragic events in life. "Who is there for me now?" I remember asking God over and over. Even though I was happily married with three wonderful children and had a full and busy life that included a large extended family, many friends, and wonderful colleagues, I felt utterly alone in the dark sea of grief.

> *Grief is extremely lonely, and very few people can imagine the pain that desperate grief causes.* —KATHLEEN, 39

But why aren't people more understanding and supportive? Certainly most of our friends and coworkers are themselves siblings. Even if they've never lost a sibling before, they must be capable of *imagining* such a loss. Why, then, don't they reach out to us during such a difficult time?

There seem to be several factors contributing to the lack of understanding and support surviving siblings receive from others. As I've already mentioned in the introduction, we live in a culture that is largely inept when it comes to condolence and other grief-related issues. Most Americans are both unschooled and uncomfortable when it comes to condolence. Moreover, the death of a sibling in adulthood, unlike the loss of a parent, a child, or a spouse, is not generally considered to be a major loss.

Further, it's fairly common for adult siblings to live in different states or even in different countries. When you lose a sibling who lives far away from you, it's more difficult for those in your immediate social circle to feel any real connection to your loss. After all, most of the people in your life have probably never met your sibling; some may not have known you even *had* a sibling.

I live in California and none of my friends there had ever met Patsy [age 45]. If I said that I was sad because my sister died, they would say, "Oh, I didn't know that you had a sister." I couldn't talk about it to people like that. A few friends actually said to me, "You should be over it by now." I found this unforgivable.
                                        —KATHY-ANNE, 53

When I returned home to Tennessee after the funeral, it was strange because no one here had known my brother, Andy [age 25]. It felt like this monumental thing was happening in my life, but only my husband could share it with me. Although people here knew about Andy, they couldn't share much in my grief. Basically, my husband was all I had. I was very touched by the few people who were thoughtful enough to send me a sympathy card. —LISA-MARIE, 34

Kathy-Anne's and Lisa-Marie's stories are very similar to the story related to me by my sister Tracy, who lived some eight hundred miles away from our brother. Although Tracy visited him occasionally, few of her friends had ever met him. When she returned from what had been the defining moment of her life (watching her only brother suffer and die), she wanted and needed to share this experience with those close to her. I recall a long conversation with Tracy in which she painfully recalled the dismissive condolences of friends and colleagues. "Now that a couple of weeks have passed," she told me one night through tears of frustration, "even my closest friends act as if nothing has happened. It's almost as if their rejection of me as a grieving person is somehow a rejection of him, and that's almost too much to bear."

Tracy accurately captures the sense of abandonment that grieving siblings often feel; friends and family members who in the past have listened, offered advice, and cared for us when the chips were down unexpectedly withdraw, distancing themselves emotionally.

Beyond my close friends, I found that most people seemed to feel uncomfortable or awkward around me after Stefani's [age 25] death. This surprised me and was disappointing. Most would either give me a strained one-liner cliché that was supposed to help me feel better, or worse, they would completely avoid discussing Stefani's death. Before experiencing Stefani's death, I probably would have acted the same way if I were in their position. I know that they meant well, but these types of reactions didn't help at all. What I needed at the time was just the opportunity to talk about Stefani's death and to know that they sympa-

thized with me. I didn't need people (especially those who had never been in my situation) to suggest what I should do to "get over this." —DEAN, 30

Initial phone calls, cards, and letters dwindle after a week or two, at precisely the time when the protective fog of denial is lifting and most survivors are in desperate need of support. The subject of loss is carefully avoided in conversation; worse, a sibling's death may be mentioned in a way that fails to acknowledge the surviving sibling's grief at all. I recall one grieving brother who said, "Lots of people mentioned my brother's death, but only in the context of those who might be closer to my brother than me and who would therefore have a 'legitimate' claim in grieving for him."

Tommy's [age 36] friends and the general public (who sent notes and tokens of love to my parents, sister-in-law, and nieces by the hundreds—God bless them!) recognize the losses of my parents and Tommy's wife and daughters. There just doesn't seem to be a socially correct way to say, "Hey, I need somebody here for me, too!" My friends were there for me to talk with, but they also saw my parents' loss as the most significant.

—KATHY B., 37

Most people don't mean to be to be insensitive; they just operate under the false notion that bringing up our loss only causes us more grief. I'm able to understand such logic now; but in early grief, it's hurtful when people avoid mentioning something that quite literally occupies nearly every thought. Grief, especially at the beginning, is beneath the surface of nearly everything we say and do. As my sister Robin once said, "I don't know why people feel like they can't mention it, since it's all I think about, anyway."

We try to be forgiving and understanding, and we try not to be angry or hurt at what feels like rejection and abandonment by the people we love. We try to reassure ourselves that people really do care; it's just that they feel awkward or clumsy when it comes to condolence. After all, we're told, most people simply don't know what to say or what to do when someone dies. But aren't these all just a mass of empty rationalizations?

The excuse of not knowing what to say to a grieving person is completely understandable for children, who often lack the emotional maturity and the appropriate communication skills that come with age. An adult, however, cannot be forgiven for using the I-just-didn't-know-what-to-say excuse for not calling, visiting, and generally being available to a bereaved friend or family member.

I don't buy for a minute the excuse that people don't know what to say. Why don't they just say, "I'm sorry for your loss"? The fact is that Americans are so afraid of death, and so unwilling to look it straight in the eye when it happens, that they shrink from it, try to minimize it, and think that they can talk it away. They refuse to face the utter pointlessness of a young person's death.

—CAROL, 42

I received several cards from people, and this was helpful; however, I did not receive one phone call from any of my friends or family. I did spend most of the first few days after Dana's [age 21] death at my parents' home, and there were several calls, many of which I answered. But not one call was ever for me, directly. I would have to say that this was kind of hard to take. My friends did come to the visitation and several were at the funeral, which was quite helpful. When I talked to them later about their initial lack of response, they said that they just didn't know what to say.

—RONNA, 34

Despite the sometimes negative or insensitive reactions of others, there are usually some people (like Clare's friends) who manage to do or say the right thing, who take the time to reach out to us and offer comfort and compassion, even if they were not personally acquainted with our brother or sister.

The most comforting thing I heard was from one of my cowork-ers. She said, "Linda, there are no rules. You feel what you feel and you act how you act." —LINDA, 51

Ask any grieving person and he or she will tell you that it is not always the people closest to you who are the most willing or able to offer support. Understanding the human limitations of those we love only adds to the pain of our loss, of course. Still, I believe human beings are bonded together by an energy we cannot see. I also believe that when we're suffering, someone invariably comes to the rescue. Our rescuer may not be a close friend or family member, but someone we barely know. I remember one such person—a kind stranger with a sympathetic smile—with great clarity.

Although I'm normally a healthy person, for about six months after my brother's death, I spent a great deal of time at the doctor's office. My health problems during this time, though numerous, were nothing serious: colds, unexplained headaches, and odd stomach upsets. During one of my many visits to the local walk-in clinic, I sat across from an elderly gentleman who had a cane resting against the chair beside him. He looked up and smiled gently as I settled myself into the seat. The waiting room was quiet; a few patients, mostly older, read magazines or watched *The Price Is Right* on the television mounted on brackets in the corner. After a few moments, the man, still smiling, asked, "You here to have your blood pressure taken?" His question surprised me. I guess he read my surprise because he inclined his head toward the sign on the door that read: "Free Blood Pressure Screening Tuesdays, 9–12."

I smiled back at him and shook my head. "No, no, I think my blood pressure is fine. I think I have another sinus infection."

He nodded as if he'd had his share of sinus problems. "Those can take a long time to clear up," he said.

"Yes," I replied, as an older woman with tight gray curls who was sitting next to me looked up from her magazine and nodded in agreement. "This is my second infection in less than a month. I feel like I've been spending a lot of time in this place lately." The old man smiled sympathetically.

For some reason, I found myself wanting to tell this complete stranger about my brother, but I suppressed the urge to do so. As if reading my thoughts, he asked, "Have you lost anyone recently?"

I was momentarily taken aback by his question, but he seemed not to notice. "I remember the year my wife died," he said quietly, now fingering his cane. "I was in here all the time with one problem or another. Grief will make you sick, you know."

"Funny you should mention that," I said softly. "My brother passed away a couple of months ago." The woman with curls put aside her magazine and made the tsk-tsk noise my mother makes whenever she hears bad news. I gave her a tight little smile, grateful for the familiar acknowledgment.

The old man stopped fidgeting with his cane and stared at the floor. "I'm sorry for your loss," he said sadly. "Your brother must not have been very old because you don't look too old."

"He was only forty-three." Another tsk-tsk beside me.

After a slight pause and a ragged little cough, the old man looked up, his light blue eyes glistening, and I knew, even before he spoke the words. "I lost a brother in 1972," he said. Then, clearing his throat, he added, "You never get over losing a brother, you know. You never really get over it."

In those few moments, in the company of total strangers, I felt more affirmation, more condolence, more genuine understanding than I had felt since my brother's death. Driving home from the clinic, I felt a little lighter, a little less alone, and perhaps a little more hopeful than I had in months.

WHAT DOESN'T HELP

I am assuming this book will be read by not only grieving siblings, but by others who care about them. In discussing the reactions of others, it seems more reasonable to begin not with what helps but instead with what doesn't. When it comes to condolence, most of us seem more adept at saying or doing the wrong thing, despite our sincere intentions to the contrary. You might recognize yourself in some of what follows and regret some things you may or may not have said or done in the past. (Of course, having experienced the death of your sibling will likely make you a more sensitive and compassionate consoler in the future—one of the few positive aspects of your present tragedy.) But the purpose here is not to condemn well-intended efforts at condolence, but to merely point out certain words and actions most surviving siblings find distinctively unhelpful.

Since the most common complaint among surviving siblings has to do with insensitive remarks, let's begin with *what not to say* to a bereaved sibling (or any grieving person, for that matter). Topping the list of things to avoid saying are such well-worn expressions as "He's in a better place" and "At least he's not suffering any more." Along the same lines, I recall several people urging me to "Cheer up. Your brother wouldn't want you to feel so sad." (Gee, if you shouldn't feel sad when your brother or sister dies, when *should* you feel sad?)

Some people were more harmful than helpful in the things they said. I became quite sick of the clichés and platitudes. A close friend of my parents', who had known Kathy [age 34] fairly well, said to me, "I guess the good Lord knew what he was doing." I responded, "I doubt that very much, but never mind." After the funeral, I introduced my husband to another old friend of my parents' and instead of expressing sorrow or sympathy, he turned to my husband and pointed to me and said, "I knew her when she was young and sweet." Understand, he wasn't talking about my dead sister . . . he was talking about me! Such idiocy is inexcusable. People who can hardly put one coherent thought together in normal times suddenly try to be as philosophical as Plato. My mother's uncle said, "Life goes on." Not for Kathy, it doesn't! My mother's cousin said, "There has to be a reason." She couldn't come up with one, however.   —CAROL, 42

Carol accurately captures the reaction most surviving siblings have with regard to what I call *pithy insights*. Pithy insights wear the costume of condolence, but in reality, such "insights" actually serve to make the speaker, not the grieving person, feel better. I recall a sister-in-law's repeated use of such insights—always of a religious nature—during a time when I had pretty much given up on believing in God. Although her attempts to offer sympathy were, I'm sure, sincere, the infantile religious imagery meant to comfort me only made me angry.

I hated people telling me that she was in a better place. The other comment I often heard that irked the daylights out of me was "Donna [age 38] would want you to carry on with your life" or "Your sister wouldn't want you to be miserable." Yeah, like that's supposed to suddenly transform my grief into a bright, sunshiny day.   —DARCEY, 37

How many times have you heard expressions like "God never gives you a burden more than you can bear" or "At least your brother/sister is at peace now"? Probably more times than you can count. Why, then, do we suddenly think those tired, worn-out clichés we've all heard a thousand times will suddenly offer comfort to someone who has just lost a brother or sister? Because we don't know what else to say, right?

> *All of the people at Patsy's [age 45] services kept asking, "Is there anything I can do?" I got so sick of hearing that question. EVERYBODY said it. Finally, I answered, "Yes! Can you bring Patsy back?" The woman I said that to was shocked.*
>
> —KATHY-ANNE, 53

As annoying and unhelpful as pithy insights may be, they are preferable to some of the more inappropriate responses cited by surviving siblings. For example, there are always people who seem almost ghoulishly interested in the details of another's death. Of course, to ask the bereaved probing questions of such a personal nature demonstrates not only a lack of social propriety, but also a complete lack of compassion for the grieving person.

> *My younger brother, Ed [age 26], died on September 11, 2001, during the attack on the Pentagon. It bothered me that mere acquaintances would ask about the gory details of Ed's death. At first they asked, "Did they find his body?" The next insult to injury: "What did his body look like?" The first time I was asked such questions, I cried. One woman said, "I didn't mean to make you cry." You could have fooled me!*
>
> —ANDREA, 31

People who feel as if they're entitled to all the grim details of your sibling's death are not genuinely interested in offering you consolation; their motives are usually selfish and result in more suffering, not less. Mourners are often blindsided by such questions at a time when they feel vulnerable and bruised anyway. This is particularly true in certain situations, such as sibling death by murder (as in Andrea's story, above, and Mary's story, which follows) and sibling death resulting from suicide.

> *Most people had no idea how to relate to my pain or what was happening. Because my sister Kathleen [age 29] was murdered along with her two young children, the news media and our town were obsessed with sensationalism. My sweet-hearted sister was a hippie and had some marijuana in her cabin, so there were certain people who said things like "She deserved it!" Wow! They would say this, even though her two young children were also murdered, in the same room with their mother.*
>
> —MARY, 52

> *A word about suicide . . . Our society truly denies death and rarely provides the proper support a bereaved person needs. Yet when a loved one dies of suicide, you feel judged by family, friends, neighbors, coworkers, and society in general. Everyone wonders what was so terrible about your family that a member would choose death over life. You feel that you must provide explanations and justification at a time when others should provide love and support unconditionally. Returning to school after Susan's [age 17] death was torture. I returned to rumors of pregnancy, drug abuse, child abuse and understood Susan's point of view . . . that life can be worse than the fear of death.*
>
> —VICTORIA, 26

Fortunately, there are very few people who inquire about the details surrounding my brother's death, which is a blessing since I'm not entirely certain just how he died. As best we can tell, he died from complications of the flu (although my mother remains convinced he had cancer). He was also HIV positive, which, of course, compromised his immune system (although, thankfully, he never developed AIDS). So when the occasional person does ask about the details of his death, I'm never quite sure how to respond. After a while, I decided that those I love already know what little I know about his death, and that the people who don't really care about me and who are inconsiderate enough to ask such questions really don't deserve a thoughtful response.

> *One man at work asked me, "How long do you think it will take to get over this?" Like it was a bad cold, to be shaken off. A friend asked me if there was anything funny, anything I could laugh at, about my sister's death (she was murdered).*
>
> —JILL, 51

Another condolence no-no is to make false promises or statements that on the surface sound very caring and sincere, but are really just fluff. A good example is the ever popular "Call me if you need me." Rest assured, a grieving person will NEVER call you. It's not that they don't need you or want you around, because they probably need all the help they can get. The reason "Call me if you need me" never works is because most grieving people simply lack the emotional energy to call and ask for help. Some feel too embarrassed, while others recognize the statement as insincere to begin with. It's probably a better idea to say something like "I'm going to call you tomorrow to see how you're doing." Better yet, decide on a time to visit, and then follow through.

> *Most people in my dealings have been the "Let me know what I can do" variety, not the "I am doing this." I needed the latter. I also had the bad luck of not having anyone who would just let me ramble on about Tommy [age 36], our childhood, and other things. People just wanted to say they were sorry, give me a hug, and then change the subject.* —KATHY B., 37

Surviving siblings also cite *story topping* as another inappropriate but common reaction from others. Story topping is usually intended as a way to commiserate with the bereaved—to try to let the grieving person know you've been there—yet story topping usually has the opposite effect. Unless you've lost a sibling under similar circumstances, it's best to avoid comparing your loss to another's, thus making their loss really about you.

My biggest problem with other people's reactions was when they would say things like "Oh, I know just how you feel. My grandfather died last month." I mean, excuse me, but your grandfather had a long life, and it was probably his time to die. My sister, on the other hand, was only 40. She had a successful law practice with a partner. She was married with a five-year-old child. None of her friends had died; she was not an old woman with little left to look forward to. How could they equate an elderly man's death with hers? Additionally, the feelings I had for my sister were extremely close; she was my oldest sibling, my best friend, and my surrogate mother. It is insensitive for anyone to think that losing a grandparent is exactly like my experience.

—J. ELIZABETH, 31

Similarly, surviving siblings find dismissive condolences unhelpful. A dismissive condolence, as mentioned in the introduction, is a lot like story topping, only worse. A dismissive condolence appears to be an expression of sympathy, but it usually just diminishes your grief. The most common dismissive condolence, "Your brother/sister died? How awful! How are your *parents?*" is probably the most difficult to bear because, in most cases, the person offering the "condolence" doesn't even know your parents. The condolence, then, is not really meant for you at all.

A dismissive condolence can also be any action that ignores or minimizes your grief, as in Debbie's case.

After my sister's death, her pastor sent a letter to my mother to help her with the loss of her daughter. This was my only sibling, but I received nothing. I know this sounds like I'm jealous, but I'm not. I just feel that people do not realize the effect a sibling's death has on the sibling left behind.

—DEBBIE, 37

Of course, Debbie's sister's pastor should know better, but Debbie's story demonstrates the need to educate others about the nature of adult sibling bereavement—that it's not only the parents who suffer. Indeed, sibling loss is a *family* tragedy that affects all members of the family circle.

Perhaps the most important thing to remember in dealing with the reactions of others is to be straightforward and honest yourself. Be aware that people say and do stupid things, usually out of ignorance rather than malice. You'd be wise to anticipate thoughtless responses and prepare a few stock responses of your own. For example, if you're really bothered by others who offer religious reasons for your loss, such as "Your sister was so special, God wanted her with Him," you might consider using the stock response, "I'm sure you see it that way."

I wanted to SCREAM in frustration with all the questions. Most of the time, I said, "I really don't feel I can discuss this right now." Or "I still get upset when I think about these things and I don't want to talk about it."

—ANDREA, 31

If someone advises you behave in a certain way during your bereavement—suggesting, for example, that you really ought to find a new hobby to "take your mind off things"—you might respond, "Thank you for your concern, but that's really not helpful." By being politely assertive, you not only help to curtail such remarks, but you can gain some measure of power during a time when you're probably feeling pretty powerless. You might even succeed in educating a few people.

WHAT HELPS

Making promises you can't keep, offering pithy insights, mini-mizing a sibling's loss, and ignoring the situation by not saying anything are by far the most common condolence mistakes we've probably all made at one time or another. But what can you do if you really do want to help?

If you can't use the old hackneyed expressions or send the standby staple—the drippy sympathy card with a preprinted verse—what can you do? First, say what you feel: "This is terri-ble! You must be heartbroken." Don't try to come up with a theological reason for an untimely death (trust me, they're aren't any) or some powerful, otherworldly explanation for why the mourner is suffering. Just be honest and sincere.

> *One of my friends gave me much help by being wise and kind enough to just be there for me, without trying to tell me how I should feel or act.* —MARY, 52

When my brother died, a friend of his called and said simply, "This really sucks. Your brother didn't deserve this, and neither do you." That was the most genuine expression of sympathy I received. Often it's the small expressions of sympathy that com-fort the most.

> *The day of the funeral, a sympathy card was delivered to the funeral home and given to me. It was from a couple who stated that they were in a car behind Gail [age 40] when the accident occurred and hoped that we didn't mind their intrusion at so difficult a time, but they thought that we might want to know that Gail did not suffer. That made us all feel much better. It was so thoughtful of them to take the time to do that. It meant a lot. I still have the card.* —HARRI, 50

What else can you do if a friend or a family member has suffered the loss of a sibling? If you're not a great condoler by phone, try sending a note, but avoid preprinted verses. Most of those cards are more insulting than comforting. Besides, it's more meaningful when you write your own message. Wait for a few weeks, and then send another note. And by all means, visit. Stop by with a gift of food and just spend time with the bereaved. Make tea. Clean the kitchen. Listen. Ask if he or she wants to go for a walk or out to lunch. Sometimes just being present is the best medicine. Wait a few days, and then stop by again. If the grieving person isn't up for a visit, be understanding, but don't be put off. Grief is a roller coaster; you may be a welcome visitor one day and an annoying intruder the next. Try not to take it personally.

Various family members and friends were very kind and supportive in numerous ways, such as by attending the memorial service and offering hugs, words of comfort, and cards with appropriate and meaningful messages. One of my distant cousins who was there told me, "I know what it's like to lose a brother," having lost her brother to a freak accident many years earlier. Three phone calls from an aunt in Indiana, who was calling on behalf of herself and other family members in that area, made me feel loved and comforted. Two best friends, one a very good listener, were supportive and sympathetic, and this, too, was very helpful. My stepchildren were kind, supportive, and helpful in listening to me and inviting me to talk about my feelings. They also invited me to various family outings, which was helpful in maintaining the balance of relationships with other people. I've been lucky to maintain as normal a life as possible through all of this.

—LINDA-LEE, 55

For most siblings, the reactions of others can best be classified as a mixed bag: a combination of comfort and avoidance that reflects the ups and downs of grief itself. What aids and comforts one person may be offensive and irritating to another. Perhaps that's why people who know us best are usually better at consoling us, although this is not always the case. Generally speaking, genuine attempts to offer condolence are almost always gratefully received. When in doubt, it's usually better to do or say something, rather than to remain silent.

> *Friends, family, and coworkers have been great to me. They helped me through the dark days and realized the grieving process never really ends. A few friends don't want to talk about death; they talk around it. A few cards were trite or had absurd reasoning, but most were caring and full of love.*
>
> —SEAN, 40

If you're a surviving sibling who has been hurt by the reactions of others, you should share these feelings with your grief partner and write about them in your grief journal. Ask yourself: Why do I find this particular reaction so upsetting? Often it's not so much the negative reaction, but rather the person(s) behind the reaction who failed to affirm or sympathize with your loss. It's hard not to feel let down by people we thought really cared.

> *Friends weren't terribly helpful. No one came to Judith's [age 31] funeral but the immediate family. Some of my friends turned out to be fair-weather friends; others were surprisingly compassionate and available.*
> —ELISE, 36

Sometimes the people who reach out to us and help us the most are people we don't commonly recognize as part of our immediate circle of friends and family (such as the old man at the doctor's office who reached out to me). This may come as a surprise to most grieving persons, but it is often the way in which new friendships begin and old ones fade. Many surviving siblings find that people who themselves have experienced a loss are better able to comfort. After all, they know what it means to grieve and how best to offer consolation.

I have a coworker friend who lost a brother thirteen years ago. We have had a lot of talks about my feelings and my insanity. She realizes my pain and often recalls times that she felt the same way. It helps so much just to be with someone who felt what I am feeling. She has been a tremendous help. —LAURA, 39

Finally, much suffering can be avoided by simply being clear and direct in asking for and accepting condolence when it's offered. In dealing with the reactions of others, try, as much as you're able, to let people know what's helpful and what isn't. Avoid wasting your energy by becoming angry and bitter because you've been let down by people who claim to care. Just realize there are some people who will step up to the plate for you, and there are others who can't even enter the ballpark.

I got the most comfort being around my immediate family. Coworkers were very helpful. My manager, who is also a close friend, really came through. She took care of my commitments for months after Sarah [age 36] died. My friends tried to be helpful and to some extent they were. It seemed to be uncomfortable for some of them to talk about death, and I understand. I got lots of calls, some more appropriate than others, but I appreciated all of them. Just the fact that someone cares about my family and me enough to take the time to contact us was a great comfort. —PAULA, 42

4

SEARCHING FOR SOLITUDE

To Go Within

Concealed grief has no remedy.

—A TURKISH PROVERB

I WAKE early these days and remain in bed, staring into the darkness. I can't close my eyes because the images come then, blinking through my thoughts like a badly spliced film: my brother, scared and very sick, trying hard to be brave as doctors poke and prod and pat him on the shoulder; the concerned faces of the nurses who hover like angels over his bedside; my family, their faces drawn in the same sort of withered misery common to all grieving people. These images, and many more, haunt me now, pecking away at my protective shell of denial until I stand defenseless in their wake. I now understand the meaning of the expression *grief stricken;* it accurately captures the punch-in-the-stomach reality I'm experiencing.

The grief is bigger than me now; it lingers around every corner, like a bully, waiting to pounce. I feel trapped, confused, and afraid. I keep expecting someone to come to the rescue, to drop from the sky in a red cape and scare off the bully, but no one seems to notice my trembling.

So I run. Instinct leads me to seek refuge in a safe place where I can begin to make sense of my loss. My safe place, my haven, is the quiet shore just off Narragansett Bay where I make an almost daily pilgrimage, just to be alone. The solitude brings relief; it becomes my shield, my healing remedy against the noise and the mindless chatter of the day that pierce my soul like a thousand tiny needles.

I suspect there must a primal force, deep within us, that draws us to the sea; day after day I walk along the water's edge hoping to still the longing that is now so much a part of my grief.

Standing on the beach, bundled warm against the cold, I'm immediately calmed by the familiar rhythm of the waves as they push toward the shore and then recede. Here, the grief seems less like a bully and more like a tentative child, peering at me from a distance, waiting for a signal to move closer. Gradually, a soft glow of peace eases its way into my soul, and, for a brief moment, I let go of the pain and cast it into the churning black waters.

One evening, as I'm about to leave the beach, I stand beside my car and admire the sun as it grazes the surface of the water in gentle descent. I'm completely absorbed in the beauty of the sunset and linger until the shadows fade into the cold winter night. I climb into the car and sit for a moment in the darkness. I have an uneasy feeling, almost as if I've forgotten something. "What is it?" I ask myself. "What *is* it?"

And then, all at once, a memory flashes.

My brother and me, two summers ago, on this very beach, watching the sun set and talking about traveling together to Israel. "Someday," he told me, "we'll go. We'll see it all: the Wailing Wall, the Dome of the Rock, the Sea of Galilee. Maybe we can even spend a few days in Egypt. I've always wanted to see the pyramids."

As he spoke, I imagined the two of us cavorting around Israel in a rented Jeep, bargaining with merchants, floating on our backs on the Dead Sea, and climbing the steep rock face of Masada. The memory is so vivid; I see his tanned profile, the tiny lines around his eyes, his hair, shaggy and bleached from the sun and the chlorine from our pool. I hear his voice, clear and strong, always with a note of reassurance. I can feel what it's like to be with him—that same easy, familiar presence I've known all my life.

And then, in an instant, it's gone. The memory vanishes as quickly as it came, slipping beneath the dark waters with the late afternoon sun.

I sit very still for several minutes, a flutter of grief rising in my chest. "How can life go on without you?" I whisper as I start the engine and head for home.

• • •

As the shock and denial that initially guides most surviving siblings through those first difficult days and weeks begins to fade, the terrible finality of death dawns. Exhaustion, grief, and confusion drive many to withdraw into a period of introspection and contemplation. We work to set the details of our sibling's death in our mind, turning over questions that have no answers: How did this happen? Did I say and do the right thing? Why my sibling? Why my family? We replay, over and over, the events of our brother's or sister's passing until they become a reality, forever sealed in our memory.

> *After making many phone calls to inform the rest of the family of James's [age 29] suicide, I retreated into many months of tears, prayers, sleep, and isolation. Whether this was a time of denial or a healing subsistence, I still cannot discern. I stayed away from people as much as possible.* —NADINE, 41

Solitude—our self-imposed seclusion—is not the same as denial, however. In denial, we cannot or will not believe our sibling is gone, or we try to fool ourselves into believing things are not as bad as they may seem. But now we *know* it's real. Sometimes this reality is so painful that we can't talk about it—even with those we love. There are no words, after all, that can express the enormity of our loss. Others, of course, may misinterpret our silence as evidence that we're moving forward, when the opposite is probably the case. In fact, one of the most ironic twists in the grief journey is likely to occur at this juncture. That is, the full impact of our brother's or sister's death begins to seep into our consciousness at precisely the same time when others might expect us to be feeling better. Hence, you'll probably begin to notice a gradual withdrawal of support just when you need it the most.

> *Others expect that you've moved on, because they have. There's a lot of initial compassion and support, but it fades quickly; most people feel as if they've already done their duty. Some may feel that to bring up your loss would be too painful for you, so they never ask how you're doing NOW. It may be months before you can actually feel the pain, and, of course, that's when you need the support most, but it's probably too late.*
>
> —KATHY-ANNE, 53

· · ·

Odd things begin to happen after the sunset on the beach; I start to see my brother in all sorts of strange places. I don't *really* see him, of course, but I *think* I see him—crossing the street in downtown Providence or looking back at me from a crowded bus as it passes. Once, I even think I see him on television as the camera pans the audience during a Celtics game.

I don't share this information with anyone because, intellectually, I know none of the look-alikes is really my brother. Just the same, I'm unnerved by these pseudosightings and spend time alone, trying to decipher their meaning. Is my mind playing tricks on me? Do I think I see my brother because I'm always thinking about him? Or am I unconsciously searching for people who resemble him? If so, why?

The shock and disbelief have given way to a sort of pining, a longing to see my brother just one more time. I find myself making a special effort to remember the little things about him, like the way he used to rake his fingers through his hair when he was frustrated or the funny way he spoke to my children, as if they were grown-ups. Perhaps this preoccupation with remembering has somehow triggered the sightings.

I knew that they were gone forever, but I would catch myself reaching for the phone to call them. Sometimes, someone looked like either Dougie [age 26] or Denny [age 23] from a distance and my heart would leap into my throat. I would stay up late, trying to figure out how I could reach out and see them just one more time. I couldn't really talk to any other family member about it because when I looked into their faces, I saw my own pain, and there was no point in talking about it. We were all going through the same thing.   —CAROLYN, 48

As unusual as it may seem, *searching behavior* and even false sightings are fairly common grief reactions. Psychologist John Bowlby understood both yearning and searching as forms of attachment behavior. Although Bowlby's work focuses primarily on parent-child relationships, his attachment theory makes a great deal of sense with regard to brothers and sisters, considering the longevity and complexity of the sibling bond. We form attachments with our brothers and sisters early in life, and these attachments generally grow deeper with age; the older you are when your sibling dies, the deeper your attachment.

Surviving siblings "search" for their deceased brothers and sisters in all kinds of places. For example, if your sibling suffered a prolonged illness and you fell into the rhythm of the hospital routine, you may find yourself going out of your way just to drive past the hospital one more time. Or you might search for your sibling in his or her neighborhood, driving past your brother's or sister's home, half-expecting him or her to walk out the door and wave a greeting. One surviving sibling confided that he often drove past the building where his brother had worked, glancing up at the fourth floor corner office his brother had been so proud to call his own, hoping to see him looking out the office window as he drove past.

Searching behavior can sometimes manifest itself in more

subtle ways. For example, I now believe the reason I feel so drawn to the beach is because I'm actually searching for my brother there, or at least a connection to him. My brother loved the beach and spent most of his adult life living on or near the water. Whenever I think of him, even today, images of him walking along the Florida shore come immediately to mind. Because we had not yet had a memorial service for him, I had no grave to visit—no place where I could go and feel connected to him. The beach is the one place where I still feel close to him, even though time is carrying him further and further away from me.

Coupled with the searching and longing, however, is the overwhelming need to be alone. The solitude feels right, like the special spot on the sofa we claim as our own. But craving solitude and actually having quality time alone can be two very different things.

During this time, my life seems overwhelmingly cluttered; caring for my family, working, cooking, even walking the dogs are all obstacles to what I really need—solitude. So I try to find relief in small ways. For instance, I keep to myself at school, eating lunch at my desk rather than in the crowded faculty room I used to love. Besides, I'm feeling increasingly uncomfortable in the faculty room these days. The other teachers have stopped asking me how I'm doing; most seem to avoid talking to me altogether. It's that tenuous time between the actual loss and what others perceive should be an end to mourning; they've extended their sympathies, but now it's time to move on. They have no idea that the real pain of my loss has only just begun.

At home, I've stopped answering the phone and glare at it when it dares to ring. I turn down lunch and dinner invitations from friends and feel almost annoyed when they think to include me in their parties or other celebrations. Can't they see I've changed? I'm not the person I was several weeks ago. Their phone calls and social gatherings seem trivial and specious. All I really want is to be left alone.

I came home to stay with my parents for a while after Scott [age 32] died. Even though we were very busy taking care of his things, and despite the fact that I still had friends in the area, I did feel very isolated from others, because I felt so different from anyone I knew. I didn't really want to go out and do things with friends because that seemed too normal, and I felt anything BUT normal. I felt like I was all of a sudden a different person, but no one would know it because I looked the same. That's a very isolating feeling—knowing that you're not who everyone else assumes you to be. As sympathetic as they were, I knew they really had no idea what an impact this had on my life.

—JULIANNE, 40

Julianne frankly describes the feelings of disconnectedness voiced by many surviving siblings. These feelings stem from the fact that we've just been through a trauma. Like Julianne, we feel different from others, changed in a way that nongrievers simply can't understand. Because of these feelings of disconnectedness, many surviving siblings find it difficult to reach out to friends and family, so they simply withdraw.

I felt isolated because there was no one in the family close to me in age or emotion with whom I could process memories and talk about how final this loss was to me. —BETTY, 76

For me, comfort comes from my daily trips to the beach and in the familiar quiet of my bedroom. The healing effects of my temporary escapes are not long lasting, however, and I find myself spending more and more time alone. I'm also consumed with an unremitting fatigue. I come home from work and fall asleep on the couch, still wearing my coat and gloves. My husband looks worried and asks, "What can I do to help?"

I tell him, "Nothing. I don't know what I need."

"I wish you'd stop shutting me out," he says. "Even when

you are here you're not here." I get his meaning, but I'm too tired to discuss it, so I just shrug and walk away.

I returned to work the next month, but I could barely make it through the day. Everyone around me told me how thin I looked (I lost ten pounds that month). Exhaustion consumed me. As soon as I got home, I didn't answer the phone or even talk with my husband. It was too much effort. All I could do was cry and then go to bed and sleep. I withdrew from everyone and just wanted to be left alone. This lasted for about a year and a half.
　　　　　　　　　　　　　　　　　　　—DEBBIE, 37

Solitude can best be understood on three basic levels: physical, emotional, and spiritual. The physical need for solitude, perhaps the most common, is characterized primarily by social withdrawal. Surviving siblings seek a quiet place away from others, a place where they are free to reflect, cry, pray, and grieve in their own unique way.

I have gone through several withdrawal periods when I just need to pull away from everyone and hide with my pain. I shut myself away, listening to our favorite childhood songs, and cry for hours.
　　　　　　　　　　　　　　　　　　　—KATHY B., 37

While this alone time seems vitally important to most mourners, there's often a strange paradox associated with physical solitude: not only do survivors want to *be* alone, they feel as if they *are* alone, which is clearly not the same thing. On the one hand, you crave physical solitude; on the other, you need the love and support of those around you. In a rather strange conflict of needs, your quest for healing space may result in actually pushing away the very people who could probably offer you the most comfort.

Emotional solitude takes many forms, from an intentional

withholding of feelings to not having anyone with whom you might share the intense and confusing emotions associated with grief. In our culture, for example, most men have been socialized not to express their feelings, especially those feelings associated with "negative" behaviors, such as crying; while other people, like Betty (see above), don't have anyone with whom they might openly express their feelings of sorrow.

In most cases, however, emotional solitude refers to the desire to simply *go within*. That is, we begin to try to come to terms with our loss. This usually involves the long process of *reorientation*—the period in which we begin to learn how to adjust to life without our brother or sister.

But how can I learn to live in a world that doesn't include my brother? All my life, I've always been my brother's sister; it's part of my identity, part of who I am. My brother is part of my past; we share a common history. And we had plans for the future. I must, therefore, shift my perspective and change many goals in order to assimilate his loss into my life. Needless to say, this is an emotionally painful process because it feels as if I'm weeding him out of my life, which only compounds my grief.

Reorientation is also taking place within my family of origin. Established roles begin to shift, and no one quite knows their place anymore. We try on new roles, but they don't quite fit; we shuck them off uncomfortably, like old coats. My sisters and I wonder: Now that our brother is gone, who will dispense wise advice to the rest of us? Who will be the life of the party, mediate quarrels between sisters, be uncle and godfather to our children? Our brother's many roles lie in a heap on the floor alongside a mound of unfulfilled dreams. My sisters and I circle the heap, surveying the devastation wrought by his passing, and then retreat, each to her own quiet place of coping.

In addition to the physical and emotional aspects of solitude, many surviving siblings find this to be a time of great spiritual awakening. Prayer takes on new meaning, and old, discarded religious rituals are often resurrected and practiced with fervor. In the quiet hours spent alone in reflection, many surviving brothers and sisters begin to establish a spiritual connection with their deceased sibling.

I sometimes think that Barbara [age 29] speaks to me when the wind blows or when the phone rings and there's no one there. I think, "Maybe she's trying to reach out to me across time."

—JERRY, 63

Religion was not big in my life before Sarah [age 36] died, but now I think about it more. Lots of people have told me their religious imagery. I have a friend who believes in reincarnation and has told me a lot about it. She thinks my niece, born seven months after Sarah's death, is Sarah's soul. I watch my niece for signs and feel a little excitement any time it seems like she recognizes something. I do not question anyone's belief about what happens after death, and I'm more curious about such things since losing my sister. I believe Sarah is still somehow connected to us.

—PAULA, 42

WHAT HELPS

Most evenings after dinner, I retreat to my bedroom, where a ritual of sorts develops. I lock the door, light several candles, and turn off the lights. Sitting cross-legged on the floor, I spend several minutes in a sort of meditation, attempting to empty my mind of all thought. Although I'm familiar with the process of meditation, I can't quite connect; I end up either falling asleep or feeling frustrated because I can't seem to clear my mind.

Eventually, I get up, blow out the candles, and turn on the lights. I reach under the bed and retrieve the small box that contains letters and cards from my brother. There aren't any photographs of my brother in the box, however; I can't bear to look at those yet. But the letters and cards bring me comfort. I reread all of them every night and then lovingly restack and tie them with a little blue ribbon.

Finally, I conclude the ritual with an attempt to record my feelings in my grief journal. At first, the pen moves furiously across the page, but then I stop abruptly and toss the journal to the floor. The writing dries up quickly. I spend the rest of the evening dozing lightly or just staring up at the ceiling. Thoughts form and fade, but I'm too exhausted to try to develop them into anything meaningful.

"This must be what happens to people just before they go crazy," I think to myself every night. But I can't change the ritual now. It's the only way I'm holding on.

Ritual has always been an important part of my life. Growing up, there were established rituals we all followed, from the normal rituals, such as saying our prayers before going to sleep and leaving cookies and milk for Santa, to the more bizarre, superstitious kinds, like the bless-yourself-whenever-you-pass-by-a-cemetery ritual to the lift-your-feet-whenever-you-drive-over-railroad-tracks-and-say-a-prayer ritual. We had rituals for everything, and we believed in them all. Rituals turned seemingly mundane events, like going to bed or driving past a cemetery, into something meaningful and sacred.

Because ritual is such an important aspect of my life, it's a natural progression for me to somehow incorporate it into my grief journey. Although my particular healing ritual might seem a little odd, I'm convinced it helped me to better cope with my loss.

If you're spending a lot of time alone, you, too, might consider creating a healing ritual for yourself. You'll probably find the repetition of ritual both comforting and empowering: comforting in the sense that the ritual is specifically for you, designed with your emotional, physical, and spiritual needs in mind, because you design it; and empowering because you're dealing with your loss in your own way during a time when you probably feel helpless and powerless. Beyond these two positive aspects, however, is a third: having an established healing ritual in place early in your grief journey can help thwart the development of destructive rituals so common during bereavement. Unfortunately, many grieving people turn to unhealthy, self-destructive rituals as a way of coping, particularly if alcohol, drugs, or food have been used in the past as coping tools.

The weekend after my brother's death, my husband said that I could get a puppy. I started drinking a lot. I felt like I had to be normal for the children (who had not known my brother or any of my family very well). I would start drinking cheap champagne as I made dinner and end up going through the whole bottle and going to bed while my husband had dinner with the children. I would wake up at one or two in the morning and go sit outside with my puppy in my lap and cry and cry. I would sit in the quiet dark and just look up into the sky and cry into my puppy's fur while going through a second bottle of champagne. Sometimes I would sit up until it was time to wake up my family and other times I would fall asleep, exhausted. I don't think that my solitude was a good thing, but I'm not sure what else I could have done. I'm a private person and not at all into girl talk or deep, personal conversations. —FRANCESCA, 43

Although your ritual should reflect your particular needs, what follows are some suggestions you may find helpful in getting started.

- Begin by first creating a specific grieving space. This can be a corner of your bedroom, a place in a spare bedroom, or in the basement—any place you can go and spend some quiet time alone. This place should be designated as your own, and you should request that other family members respect and stay away from your grief space. You should also let family members know when you need some peace and quiet and ask for their loving cooperation in helping you to heal. You might even consider making a sign to hang on the door to remind others not to interrupt your alone time.

- You can personalize your grief space by decorating it with flowers, candles, photographs of your sibling, religious symbols, or any other object that brings you comfort. Many also find aromatherapy beneficial, especially in the form of candles (or, if you prefer, oils or incense). Melissa, clary sage, frankincense, sandalwood, cedarwood, lavender, and benzoin are particularly helpful in relieving stress and are therefore conducive to creating the peace of mind necessary for contemplation. Most of these products are available online (see "Chapter Resources" in the appendix).

- You can further enhance your experience by playing music, such as soothing classical tunes or New Age sounds. If you're like me and prefer something more contemporary and evocative, I have a few suggestions. First, my favorite sound track is from the movie *City of Angels* (Peter Gabriel's "I Grieve," Sarah McLachlan's "Angel," and U2's "If God Will Send His Angels" are exceptional). Second, the little-known artist Eva Cassidy, who herself suffered an untimely death from melanoma at age thirty-three, seems to sing to the soul of the bereaved in *Songbird* and *Eva by Heart*. Her renditions of "Fields of Gold" and "Over the Rainbow" are lovely, but it's her song "I Know You by Heart" that especially resonates with surviving siblings (all three songs can be found on her *Songbird* album). Finally, Amy Grant's heartfelt "I Will Remember You" from her album *Heart in Motion* captures many of the feelings you're probably feeling right now.

How long do most surviving siblings feel the need to actually use a grieving space? Although this varies greatly from sibling to sibling, I think it's a good idea to have a special place to which you can withdraw for about a year. Of course, you may find that having a space to call your own offers benefits that extend beyond the grief work originally intended. If this is the case, you might decide to make your space a permanent fixture.

> *My brother, Peter [age 36], was a national sailing champion. I placed one of his large trophies on a stand and hung his photograph along with a poem written about him in my home. The "shrine" served its purpose for about a year, and then I found it was no longer necessary and took it down.* —K. M. G., 43

Although the creation of a grieving space and a grieving ritual can be helpful, too much of a good thing can be detrimental. While it may seem easier to shut out the world and withdraw from uncaring people, responsibilities, and the general frenzy of day-to-day living, balance is really the key. Continue to set aside time each day for yourself, but remember, there are those who care about you and genuinely want to help you through this difficult time.

> *I retreated from most of the outside world for about a year. I lived alone with my eight-year-old daughter and became more protective of her than I was naturally. Sometimes, solitude is very helpful and necessary, but too much of it can become a web that is very difficult to pull out of.* —MARY, 52

• • •

For me, having time alone becomes an essential part of my journey. I experience a liberating feeling in being able to grieve in my own way, away from the worried, watchful eyes of family members and friends.

But the price of solitude is high.

Sitting in my driveway late in the afternoon, waiting for the car to warm up, I see my children through the family-room window, huddled together under a blanket, watching television. A shadow of guilt approaches and taps my shoulder. "You're so selfish," whispers the shadow. "How can you even think of leaving those children again?" I struggle for a moment between the two forces—guilt and my need for solitude—and, in the end, I accept both. The shadow sits beside me in the passenger seat as I shift into reverse, back out of the driveway, and head to the beach.

If you're like me, you may struggle simply to find the time to be alone. You may feel guilty for trying to take care of yourself, and you may decide that the guilt isn't worth the price you have to pay for solitude. I hope you don't arrive at this decision, because I truly believe that unless you find some time for yourself, your grief will likely intensify. If you're having troubling finding time to be alone, rework your priorities and *make* time. If you're feeling too guilty to honor your need for solitude, try explaining your needs to those around you and enlist their support. Even young children will cooperate if you're clear about how important this is to you. If you're a parent, remember that the benefits of solitude will actually make you a better parent in the long run, so let go of the guilt and make some time for yourself.

I do have a word of caution with regard to solitude, however. Friends and family may express concerns about your need to withdraw. While these concerns, in most cases, are probably unwarranted, remember that social withdrawal is often a symptom of depression, a serious medical condition that requires immediate attention (see chapter 7 for more on depression). Try to be clear, then, about your reasons for seeking solitude and certainly report any unusual symptoms to your physician.

I withdrew from some of my family and friends. I was out of my head with grief. I think that solitude is necessary, but it would have been harmful for me to have spent too much time alone. I still have a hard time being alone. I remember reading that the only way through this is to reach out to other people. If you stay overwhelmed with your own pain and don't reach out, I think the battle is lost. —KATHLEEN, 39

Generally speaking, if you're staying away from others to such a degree that your work and family life suffers, it can be an indication that you're stuck and in need of a little push. Although I'll discuss grief therapy in more detail in chapter 7, it's important for you to keep both individual and group therapy as an option at any stage of your journey. Try to think of grief counseling more as a safety net, rather than an indication of some deep-seated neurosis. Not everyone feels they can benefit from therapy, but when you're stuck, it's a helpful option.

Aside from the general concern others may have about your need to be alone, there will be some who misinterpret solitude as evidence of your failure to get over your loss. Remember that most people operate under the false assumption that grief is something we have to let go of and so they're likely to be short-sighted when it comes to time allotted for mourning. These are the people who may urge you to get back into a regular, productive routine, believing that this will somehow make your grief less painful. "Just go back to work and try to put all of this behind you" is the advice I received from more than one friend. Although such advice may be helpful to some, the point should be made that when we hurry grief along on someone else's timetable instead of our own, we run the risk of stuffing our feelings rather than dealing with them. The result, as in Rosemary's case, can add to the misery of our loss.

I kept to myself, away from my husband, for about a year. I hated him for not allowing us to visit my brother in various parts of Europe where he lived because of our budget. I cried all of the time. I gained weight and stopped running in races. I thought that I, too, would have a heart attack. My husband and I eventually divorced. On one of our last evenings together, I was sobbing after seeing a movie about a murder at West Point [Sean, 43, had graduated from West Point] and my husband yelled, "Hey! Are you ever going to get over the death of your brother?"
—ROSEMARY, 51

Finally, continue to do what feels right for you. Whether it is wearing an external sign of mourning, writing in your grief journal, creating a grief space, or taking daily walks with your grief partner, just know that your primary task right now is simply to remain in touch with your feelings.

It was difficult to be around normal (nongrieving) people. Their lives seemed so placid and pain free. I decided to take a seven-month leave of absence from work and to try to relax, travel a bit, and recover. I guess the solitude was useful in that I didn't have to put on a happy face when I wasn't feeling that way.
—JILL, 51

Over time, as your need for solitude gradually diminishes, you're likely to feel irrevocably changed by your loss. This is not some strange aspect of grief, but rather a universal truth. Ask anyone who has lost a brother or a sister and they'll tell you: "I'm not who I used to be." Every loss changes us; you'll never be the person you were before your brother or sister died. Once you accept this, you can let go of the fantasy that things will eventually return to the way they used to be and get on with the hard work of finding meaning in your loss and then integrating it into your life.

And don't be surprised if the time spent alone leaves you with some nagging questions to which there are no satisfying answers. You may find yourself wrestling with such weighty matters as the meaning of life and the seemingly incongruous connection between God and the suffering of an innocent person. As these and other questions predominate your thinking, the injustice of it all seems too much to bear. And that's when you get mad.

5

ANGER

How Dare This Happen!

Since brass, nor stone, nor earth, nor boundless sea,
But sad mortality o'ersways their power,
How with this rage shall beauty hold a plea,
Whose action is no stronger than a flower?

—WILLIAM SHAKESPEARE

I SIT AT the kitchen table and open a card from a neighbor who has heard the news that my brother died. It's a religious card. Parted clouds and bright rays of sun beckon a single white dove upward. The words *With Sympathy*, etched in gold script, banner the top of the card. I open it and read the singsongy printed verse within that is somehow supposed to be uplifting. A message of condolence has been scribbled beneath: "I know that you and your brother lived far away from one another," it reads, "but I know that he was always close to your heart." I feel anger burning up my neck and into my cheeks as I read on. "I hope it comforts you to know that he is at peace." I stare at the card and reread the message. Now I'm furious. I toss the card across the table and mutter, "Bullshit." My husband, sitting across the table and working on bills, picks up the card now lying in front of him and asks, "Is something wrong?" I look at him and respond sarcastically, "No dear, everything is just great." Assuming that the card must contain some sort of insult, he reads it and then looks back at me, confused.

"That card is bullshit," I remind him. He looks at the card to see if he's missed something and asks, "What is it about this card that has you so upset?" I can't believe he can be so obtuse. "Just look at it!" I shout, wagging a finger at the offensive card. "I *am* looking at it," he replies. "What's wrong?" I draw a long, exasperated breath and tell him, "It's a stupid religious card with a hackneyed verse about trusting in God." My husband smiles and says gently, "Well, you *do* teach religion. I'm sure the card was meant to be comforting." I am amazed to hear him say such a ridiculous thing. I stand up and snatch the card from his hand and read the contents in my best pretend-preacher voice. When I finish, I read the inscription in mock sympathy: "I know that you and your brother lived far away from one another but I know that he was always close to your heart." I pause and glare at my husband. "I hope it comforts you to know that he is at peace." My husband comes toward me, hand outstretched, eyes filled with compassion. For some reason, this makes me even angrier.

I tear the card in half and throw it on the floor. "Talk about a minimizing condolence! And for the record," I shout, the quick, hot tears of anger burning in my eyes, "it's *not* a comfort to know that my brother is at peace, whatever *that* is! I'd rather have him here with me, thank you!" I'm sobbing now and my head is pounding. I know I'm acting like a six-year-old, and the rational voice of reason whispers restraint. I ignore it; instead, I want to overturn the table and break every dish in the house. I push my chair roughly to the side and say, "And I don't need stupid people sending me stupid cards that try to make a bad thing seem like it's not really so bad!" I run from the room and lock myself in the bathroom. My speechless husband picks up the torn card and places it in a drawer along with the others. He returns to the bills and waits for the storm to pass.

Alone in the bathroom, I'm so angry I could spit. I stomp around the room for several minutes, ranting and raving. My younger son, Jack, knocks on the door and asks me if I'm playing. Playing? *Playing?* I start to tell him to go away and leave me alone, but the way he asked the question strikes me as oddly funny and I start to laugh. I catch sight of myself in the mirror—mascara-streaked tears glistening my cheeks, a lopsided smile, my hair a wild, neglected tangle. "I think I've lost my mind," I tell my reflection. "I might even care about that if I weren't so goddamn angry."

I'm completely unprepared for the anger that comes several weeks after losing my brother. I'm aware that anger is a legitimate grief reaction, but I assume that I'm too sad to feel much of anything other than abject misery. Looking back on the incident that triggered this, it will come to seem ridiculous to me. I will never be entirely certain why that particular card set me off in the first place. But I remained angry for several weeks; even the dogs tiptoed around me.

The anger experienced by surviving siblings takes many forms. Some siblings feel anger at the disease or accident that claimed the life of a brother or a sister, while others may feel anger at the deceased sibling for dying in the first place. Many surviving siblings are angry with doctors and the health care system for not saving their sibling. Anger at God for allowing such a terrible thing to happen also seems to be common.

Some surviving siblings report that their anger is directed primarily at an unresponsive community of people (friends, coworkers, neighbors, and family) who fail to acknowledge the depth of their grief. This lack of social recognition, as we have already pointed out (see chapter 3), is an important factor in dealing with adult sibling loss in general.

> Most of my friends pretty much quit concerning themselves with my grief within a few weeks, maybe even sooner, days. They didn't bring Dana [age 21] up in conversation, unless, of course, I did. Then they would just politely listen. I don't want to sound unfair, but I would have to say that my biggest support came from my mom and from one friend of Dana's (whom, I must say, had actually been close to our family as she and Dana had grown up together). Unfortunately, I can't say that my husband was that great about it, either. I think that he had a certain amount of time in his mind that I should grieve and then it should be over.
> —RONNA, 34

Perhaps the most difficult form of anger we surviving siblings experience is directed at ourselves. This is particularly true in certain types of deaths, such as suicide, but most surviving siblings experience some form of self-recrimination following the death of a brother or a sister. In any case, anger at self, God, your brother or sister, doctors, the community, or the circumstances of your sibling's death seems to surface fairly quickly during the bereavement process. In fact, some surviving siblings feel anger almost from the start. You may have a single focus of your anger (like the doctor who failed to make your sibling well), or, more commonly, your response may be a somewhat twisted jumble of anger on a variety of levels.

The anger experienced by surviving siblings is in many ways similar to the emotions experienced by parents who lose a child in adulthood. In the same way that our parents feel the need to protect us, we siblings often feel it's our responsibility to protect our brother or sister, particularly if we're older. Surviving siblings often react similarly to their bereaved parents in the amount of guilt and anger they may feel over what they perceive as their failure to protect their sibling.

There is a pervasive feeling of injustice connected with most deaths, but those deaths that seem to violate the natural order of life are particularly hard to take. We fully expect our grandparents and parents to predecease us, for example. This does not mean that the loss of our grandparents and parents is any easier, only that losing our grandparents and parents is to be expected. But our brothers and sisters are supposed to help us cope with the eventual loss of our parents, grandparents, and other older relatives. Our brothers and sisters are not supposed to die until we've had the chance to grow old with them; it's the natural order of life. In some cases, as in L. B.'s story, we feel abandoned by our deceased sibling. We must now face the burden of caring for our parents alone; moreover, we will eventually have to endure the pain of our parents' deaths without the special support only siblings can provide.

After the initial shock wore off, I was angry at him. Why didn't he take better care of himself? "Now," I thought, "Paul [age 48] has left me all alone to take care of everything. Not only do I have to worry about Dad [who suffers from Alzheimer's and Parkinson's] but I now have to take care of everything." Why did he allow his medical insurance to lapse? I was looking forward to shared times in the future, after we both retired. I thought, "What a waste." —L. B., 55

Many surviving siblings express anger toward what they view as a *preventable death*. Preventable deaths include (but are not limited to) deaths from the reckless or irresponsible behaviors of a person or persons that result in the death. For example, if your sibling chooses to drink and drive, and then perishes in a fatal crash, you might feel a great deal of anger at him or her for exercising such poor judgment. Of course, as siblings, we are often in the unique position to know our brother's and sister's weaknesses. If our sibling has a problem with drugs or alcohol, chances are we know about it. We may have even delivered a lecture or two to our brother or sister on this topic, and we are likely to feel a great deal of anger if drugs or alcohol prove to be a factor in our sibling's death.

We will undoubtedly feel a certain amount of guilt in the previous scenario, especially if we feel partly responsible for our sibling's death, or if we feel that our sibling brought on his or her own demise, as in Lisa-Marie's story.

The last day of Andy's [age 22] life was spent drinking alone. What a stupid and selfish thing to do! He fell asleep in a drunken stupor, with his feet in the icy waters of the river. Now we are left to clean out his apartment, bury him, and explain to his six-month-old daughter where her daddy is. What a damned idiot! It was the ultimate act of selfishness.

—LISA-MARIE, 34

But what happens when the lines between our sibling's irresponsibility and our own sense of irresponsibility are not so clear? We are unlikely to experience this blurring of the lines in other deaths, but because of the close relationship, it is somehow easier for us to feel some amount of responsibility for a sibling's death, even if those feelings are displaced. In other words, we often tend to blame ourselves, both when there is a legitimate reason to do so (we drive drunk and an ensuing accident claims the life of our sibling, who is a passenger) and even when there's not, as in Victoria's case.

> *I arrived home at 1:00 A.M. after celebrating St. Patrick's Day with my boyfriend. I knew immediately that something was wrong. The street was filled with familiar cars. My father came out of the house to meet me and my heart pounded. I was sure that my eighty-eight-year-old grandfather had died. When I learned that it was not my grandfather, but my sister, Susan [age 17], my legs gave out and I hit the floor. I screamed, "It's not true! Did you go and see her? It's not her!" When I thought that I could not feel any more physical or emotional pain, I learned that Susan had committed suicide with my father's gun. There is only one person I cannot forgive for this tragedy: myself. I fought with Susan nearly every day of her life. I never accepted her for who she was, and I always tried to change her. My little sister was in a tremendous amount of emotional pain, and I abandoned her. I have accepted that I will always feel guilty for her death . . . it has been eight years now.*
>
> —VICTORIA, 26

Victoria blames herself for her sister's death based on the faulty perception that she somehow caused her sister to make the decision to end her life. Although Susan's death is certainly categorized as a preventable death (there is no more preventable a death than suicide), realistically, Victoria is not in any way

responsible for the decision that Susan made. Yet those old familiar feelings of sibling guilt seem to surface almost immediately.
As brother or sister, we often feel as if we, of all people, should
have been aware of our sibling's suffering. How could we *not*
know of our sibling's desperation? This is especially true in the
case of siblings who communicate on a regular basis. We may
question not only our perception of reality, replaying conversations in our head, or searching for hidden messages that we might
have missed, but we may blame ourselves unnecessarily for not
taking the kind of action that might have prevented our sibling's
death in the first place. Needless to say, sibling survivors of suicide often are left with intense feelings of anger at the thought
that their sibling intentionally chose to die and that the suffering
they are now experiencing was entirely preventable.

I use the example of suicide only because the issues of preventability and responsibility are so obvious. Surviving siblings
may, however, have similar anger reactions in other instances. For
example, if your sibling complains of feeling tired, you may
assume that he or she is working too hard. If your sibling dies the
next day, you may then feel angry at yourself for not having sug-
gested that your brother or sister see a doctor.

The subsequent anger and guilt that often result from a preventable death are therefore clouded in the case of sibling
bereavement. You'd probably feel less anger if the circumstances
surrounding your sibling's death were *not* preventable. For example, if your brother or sister died in a flash flood, you'd realize
that natural forces took the life of your sibling and nothing could
be done. Not that this type of death is any less painful, but there
is likely to be less anger associated with it.

· · ·

Two months after my brother died, I visit my parents. After dinner, my mother and I sit in silence, watching the evening news.
Images of school shootings, suicide bombers, and child killers

flash across the screen—story after story of people hurting one another and destroying lives. After a few minutes, my mother, still focused on the television screen, says quietly, "It's so unfair." I know exactly what she is talking about. I, too, have been wondering how it is that we can live in a world where murderers live long lives and decent, loving people like my brother die in the prime of life. Sitting in the darkness next to my grieving mother, I feel the anger growing, like some hideous black tumor in the pit of my stomach; it curls its ugly fingers around my heart and squeezes hard. Suddenly, I want to scream, and I barely suppress my overwhelming urge to smash the television screen to bits. My knees shake; I clench my teeth and ball my fists. Slowly, I turn my head to look at my mother, who is watching me. She looks me straight in the eye and I can see that she, too, is mad as hell.

Our anger at what we perceive as a preventable death can also extend to organizations. In fact, a number of siblings (like Clare) feel angry at various organizations whom they believe are responsible, at least in part, for the death of their brother or sister.

> *My brother's senseless joining of Alcoholics Anonymous was his initial, obviously self-destructive act. Of course, it is staffed and run by laypeople who are in no way qualified to diagnose or treat any disease at all, so his suicidal depression went undetected and untreated. Every time I hear or read about how wonderful AA is, all of my half-healed scars rip open and I feel furious all over again. I also feel some anger at my mother. Clearly, she knew that Andy [age 27] had been tangled up with them, while the veil of secrecy under which AA operates prevented the rest of us from knowing until it was too late. Why? Why didn't she get him to a psychotherapist for a proper diagnosis? Suicidal depression need not be a killing disease anymore. I am still tormented by the questions, but I suppose "why" is the ultimate question all survivors of suicide ask . . . about everything.* —CLARE, 40

Clare's anger is a mixture of anger at an organization she feels contributed to her brother's death and anger at her mother, her brother, and, perhaps, even herself. In Darcey's case, she feels a great deal of outrage at the state of Hawaii and at what she believes is an example of blatant negligence.

My sister died in a rockslide at a popular tourist attraction while visiting me in Hawaii. I was and still am furious at the state of Hawaii for promoting and allowing tourists to go into that death trap. How many tourists need to be killed or injured? I'm upset that the rescue crews that eventually arrived did not have adequate lifesaving devices. I am angry that they did not get to the victims sooner. I am upset at my boyfriend for tying up the phone lines with his computer, as I know that Donna [age 38] probably tried to call me that day. If the phone line hadn't been engaged, we would have spoken and the whole outcome of the day might have been different. I'm also mad at myself for not giving Donna an extra-long hug the day before she died. As we said our good-byes, we gave each other a quick peck on the cheek and a hug. I had no idea that would be the last time I ever saw her again. —DARCEY, 37

When a sibling dies from so-called natural causes—that is, an illness or a disease that could not be successfully treated by the doctors to whom we turn for healing—many siblings express anger at the medical profession. Surviving siblings cite the general insensitivity of doctors and other health-care workers as a source of anger, but most are angry because those charged with caring for a beloved brother or sister fail to make them well. Kathy-Anne, a surviving sibling, feels that doctors were directly responsible for her sister's death. "I was angry, and still am, at the doctors," she says. "I feel that they killed Patsy. I don't think that they knew how serious her condition was or how to treat it." While some may view this anger as irrational (doctors, after all, are only human), it is nonetheless quite common to focus our anger and disappointment on doctors. This anger can be very intense and can even lead to legal action, whether warranted (in cases of malpractice) or not.

Of course, if you feel that a physician directly contributed to your sibling's death and you pursue legal action against that physician or hospital, then you are likely to experience a prolonged period of anger. Trials of this nature can go on for months; the pretrial activities and appeal process even longer. All of this comes, of course, at a time in your life when you are grieving. Needless to say, legal woes can greatly frustrate the process of bereavement.

In Helen's case, it was more the blatant apathy of JoAnn's doctor that contributed to Helen's anger, leaving her with lingering thoughts of issues surrounding preventability.

> *I was (and continue to remain) angry at the medical profession. When JoAnn [age 54] first started to feel ill a few days before her death, her husband tried to get assistance from her doctor. Her doctor, however, insisted that JoAnn go into his office so that he could examine her. Her extreme obesity, however, made this virtually impossible (she weighed over six hundred pounds at her death), as it was difficult for her to get into the car. I really believe that her husband should have insisted that the doctor send someone to the house to check on her. It may have been too late at that point to do anything for her, but because the doctor didn't take the situation seriously enough, I feel that she may have died unnecessarily. What they could have done, I don't know, but the fact is, nothing was done for her.* —HELEN, 46

Sometimes surviving siblings direct their rage at their deceased sibling for getting sick in the first place. I recall a conversation with one grieving sister who said, "I know that I shouldn't say this, but if my brother had only taken better care of himself, we would not all be going through this right now." She felt immediately ashamed for blaming her brother for the illness that took his young life, but confessed, "I can't help it. I'm mad at him for being so careless about his health and all of the suffering it has brought to the family." Sometimes, as in Laura's story, it's difficult to pinpoint the actual source of our anger.

I know that I felt angry, but I do not remember whom I was angry at. I wanted to blame someone, but I did not know whom to blame. Months after my sister Sarah [age 36] died, I had a dream that made me realize that I had been angry with her. It was very hard for me to admit that, and I kept it inside for a long time. I was angry at one of my sisters for doing so much research and then calling me with updates every minute of every day, and I was angry at myself for being well. After Sarah's death, I was angry at my parents for not informing me that she was about to die until it was too late for me to get to her in time. I will always be angry about that, but will try not to let my feelings hurt my parents. —LAURA, 39

Siblings are good at being mad at one another. We are experts in pushing each other's buttons. It is often a pattern with siblings—get mad, fight, forget it. This pattern is first played out in childhood, often in the form of rivalries or other types of competition, and we feel anger and resentment when we lose. Arguments and fights break out, insults are exchanged, noses may even be bloodied, and we swear that we will never speak to our brother or sister again for the rest of our lives. The next day, however, we sit beside our brother or sister and watch television, sharing a bowl of popcorn, or we ask them to play tag or hide-and-seek, and all is forgotten. As adults, many siblings continue the same pattern of anger and forgiveness that they learned as children. Most of us would never treat others the way we treat our siblings; indeed, few relationships could withstand the sometimes topsy-turvy nature of the sibling relationship.

I recall a recent discussion I had with my good friend Nancy R. Early one morning, she called me near tears and related a terrible argument she'd had with her older brother, John, over the telephone. There was name-calling, and insults were exchanged. The argument ended abruptly when her brother hung up on her. Nancy was beside herself. Two days later, I spoke to Nancy and asked her if anyone was coming to her home to share Passover with her. "Of course," she said. "My brother John and his family will be here."

Is it any wonder, given the volatility of sibling love, that we might feel anger at a brother or a sister for dying? How dare they die and leave us! We feel angry, but there is no recourse, so we usually end up feeling guilty.

We may also feel anger at others—other family members, in particular: our parents, if they are still alive; our other siblings; assorted relatives—all of whom may be sources of potential conflict. Naturally, any conflicts you may already have with other family members can intensify during this stage of grief. You may feel anger toward family members who may have made life more difficult for your deceased sibling in the past, feeling that some of these old wounds have been reopened.

I wasn't really angry at JoAnn [age 54] herself. She died of heart failure due to morbid obesity, but I simply cannot blame her for not taking better care of herself. I know the pain she must have been in, and I understand some of the causes that led to her condition. If anything, I'm extremely angry at our (deceased) mother, who always made food such a provocative issue when we were growing up. She always commented on what we ate and how much, and she would hide food where only she (my mother) could find it. She constantly berated both my sister and me for our weight problems. —HELEN, 46

Not only must we deal with the anger associated with childhood pain, but we must also deal with anger associated with our sibling's *other family*. We are usually quite used to dealing with the collective baggage of our childhood; after all, our siblings were with us during that time, and we share a common history. Dealing with in-laws, however, is another story. If your brother or sister has a family, you may feel pushed aside; or, as in Tami's case, the focus of your anger may be someone in your sibling's other family.

A week before Bob [age 33] died, his wife told him that she was leaving him and wanted a divorce. Even though his condition may not have been treatable or associated with stress, I blamed his wife for the pain that he was going through. I felt this pain caused the aneurysm to burst. I will never forget how she made his last few days so painful and sad. —TAMI, 26

Tami's anger at her sister-in-law, by her own admission, is more about how the pending divorce made her brother's last days painful and sad. It is difficult, then, in cases such as Tami's to move beyond the anger directed at peripheral family members because there is little chance of resolution.

We may also feel anger at others, outside the family, who seem to be oblivious to our suffering. In the opening of this chapter, I discussed the anger that resulted from a card I received from a lovely, caring neighbor. Initially, I felt anger at the wording of the card, believing it to be a dismissive condolence and therefore insulting. I now realize, however, that my own need simply to feel angry at the injustice of my brother's death was the real reason for my outburst. The card was simply the catalyst. Having said this, however, I think it's important to realize that because our grief is so often minimized by society, we are more sensitive to dismissive condolences. Other people simply fail to recognize the depth of our grief, and they sometimes inadvertently say things that make us angry. Usually, it is the cumulative effect of several insensitive comments that triggers our anger.

> *One of the things I've found hard to deal with is when friends, who in many cases are otherwise sympathetic, will complain about their brother or sister: how they are not doing what they should, or behaving badly this way or that. They don't realize what it sounds like to someone like me, who lost her only brother; that I would give anything to able to have an argument with Scott [age 32] today, or see him, even once a year, or just be able to talk to him on the telephone. Even after five years, it still makes me angry when people unthinkingly talk that way about their siblings.*
> —JULIANNE, 40

When I think back to my own feelings of anger following my brother's death, I am faced with a somewhat peculiar reality. Like many other surviving siblings, I felt most of the same feelings of anger: anger at doctors, the community, family members, my brother, and even myself. But I was *most* angry with God. This admission makes me slightly uncomfortable because I have spent a good part of my life studying theology and religion; I presently teach religious studies at a small Catholic university. The expectation is that I should know better than to blame God for my brother's death and that I should not be angry with God. Intellectually, I understood that God had nothing to do with my brother's death, but I could not shake the feeling that God had let me down. I felt betrayed and angry, and I felt that way for a very long time. Like Kathy-Anne, I had trouble understanding why God should allow such an awful thing to happen to my brother and my family.

I was angry at God for allowing this to happen. I kept asking,
"Why Patsy [age 45]?" She had two small children to raise and
important work to do. I was angry at death in general. Why is
there such a terrible thing as death? Of course, I realized that
people do have to die, but I need and love my sister and could not
imagine how the world could go on without her.

—KATHY-ANNE, 53

Coupled with the anger is usually fear. I found myself reverting to a five-year-old mentality, worrying that God would punish me for feeling so angry at him. After all, if God could take my brother, who was a far kinder person than I, what was to stop God from wreaking further havoc in my life? Concerns about the health and safety of my children, my husband, my parents, and my other siblings began to surface. I was suddenly very preoccupied with death and felt as if it lurked everywhere. I have since learned that blaming God and feeling angry at God are typical grief reactions; I am also reassured that many bereaved persons experience obsessive worries about the well-being of loved ones following the death of someone close. At the time, however, these feelings were disturbing and certainly tested my faith.

Although a normal part of the grief process, anger is probably one of the most difficult emotions surviving siblings may experience. We live in a culture in which we lack the proper tools to deal with and express our anger. Women are often taught not to express anger (nice girls don't yell) while men, on the other hand, are usually schooled in inappropriate expressions of anger and rage (fighting and abusive language). Both men and women can suffer from repressed or misdirected anger, which invariably becomes self-destructive, and most surviving siblings feel a sense of relief when the intensity of this stage of grief subsides. Although anger is likely to resurface every now and again in connection with your bereavement, I hope you will eventually learn to accept your feelings of anger as one more aspect of the complex emotional journey of grief. Perhaps Paula expresses this most clearly.

> *I was angry at Sarah for smoking, which made me feel guilty. I was mad at myself for not making her take better care of herself. I think that anger is the hardest emotion to deal with. You feel angry, and then you feel guilty for being so mad. Lately, I have been thinking, "My thirty-six-year-old sister died!" Anger is a normal feeling. I have started to accept the feelings as part of all of this.*   —PAULA, 42

WHAT HELPS

Anger is such an intense emotion that most of us have trouble dealing with it under normal circumstances; when coupled with loss, it can often be the most confusing and difficult aspect of the grief process. So what can you do to help yourself work through the feelings of anger that are likely to accompany the death of a brother or a sister?

By now, I hope that you have come to rely on your grief partner and that the two of you have established a way of communicating that is both healthy and healing. Likewise, your grief journal can be a valuable source for the expression of anger. There are several other things that may be helpful to you right now as you grapple with anger.

You might consider joining a grief support group, if you have not done so already. Expressing your anger in such a forum can be immensely beneficial and you are likely to gain insight into the source of your anger (are you angry at your sibling? doctors? God? yourself?). The truth is, many surviving siblings feel so angry that often they're unable to unpack the anger to get at the true source. Knowing why you are angry is the first step in coping with it. If you are uncomfortable in a group setting, you might consider individual grief therapy; but remember, be certain that your therapist has experience in grief counseling (see chapter 7 for more information on locating a competent grief therapist).

I found exercise, in the form of walking, to be helpful during this stage of grief. Much research has been done that supports the benefits of exercise with regard to mental health. Positive endorphins that are released during even moderate exercise are beneficial in counterbalancing the adrenaline that accompanies anger. Although my anger was usually more like mild agitation, I quickly learned that a twenty-minute walk would help me to feel calmer, thereby enabling me to avoid an escalation from mild agitation to a full-blown episode of anger.

One surviving sibling told me that playing basketball is very therapeutic in dealing with anger. The pounding of the ball while dribbling can be a great stress releaser! Almost any form of exercise is likely to be helpful in dealing with anger, but the trick seems to be consistency. With this in mind, you might consider setting aside twenty minutes each day for some sort of exercise. It's probably a good idea to have some amount of exercise every day in any case, but you will reap the added benefit of a reduction in anger and anxiety when you exercise during a period of bereavement.

Meditation and yoga offer similar benefits. You can learn to meditate on your own (*Meditation Made Easy*, by Lorin Roche, is an excellent beginner book, for instance), or you can sign up for a course in meditation, sometimes offered by yoga instructors. Yoga is another great way to combat anger and reduce stress. Again, you can teach yourself yoga (you might start with *The American Yoga Association's Beginner's Manual*, by Alice Christensen), but I recommend joining a beginner's yoga class. The atmosphere of a yoga class promotes relaxation through music and affirmation. Such a class can be a respite from grief and help to redeem you from some of the isolation associated with bereavement.

You might also consider using herbal supplements, many of which are helpful in treating mild anxiety and some of the anger symptoms you may be having. Before using any herbal supplement, however, be sure to check with your doctor and pharmacist. I also recommend that you take your time in selecting a good herbalist and be sure to read up on herbal medicines in general before taking them (*The Healing Herbs: The Ultimate Guide to the Curative Power of Nature's Medicines*, by Michael Castleman, is easy to understand, even for the novice).

One thing that really helped me get through anger was to avoid people I knew would upset me. You know who they are: the people who have not been supportive of you, who minimize your grief, or who make you feel as if your grief is unwarranted.

A direct quote from my mother-in-law to my husband was "Well, it's been two months. What's wrong? Debbie should be over this by now." This made me very angry because I then knew that there was no way that she could understand what I was going through. —DEBBIE, 37

My advice to Debbie is this: Stay away from your mother-in-law right now. It's hard to believe that some people can be so uncaring at a time when you are so vulnerable, but I'm certain you'll have run into a few by now. Don't expect such individuals to understand, much less affirm, your loss. Surround yourself with people who care and want to help you during this difficult time. It is especially important now for you to avoid people likely to trigger your anger, as you're almost certain to react to them in a way you'll later regret. Chances are that if these people are insensitive enough to incite your ire in the first place, they are probably pretty unforgiving, too! No matter how difficult they might be, you certainly don't want to be estranged from friends or family members once you move beyond this intense period of grief. I've had this experience in my own grief journey, and trust me, it should be avoided at all costs.

Of course, most of these suggestions hinge on the premise that anger in grief is necessarily something to be avoided. Sometimes anger can actually serve to energize one in a positive direction.

Anger helped me act as an advocate for Eddie [age 34] in his remaining days when he wasn't able to do so for himself, as well as helped in my own emotional well-being. Anger helped me to mobilize and energize at those times when the situation called for such. While anger is not as socially acceptable an emotion as sadness or depression in grieving people (especially women), anger had a definite time and place and importance in my grieving process. —THERESA, 36

The fact is, anger is usually perceived to be less socially acceptable for women than it is for men. Our anger is often attributed to hormones or some other type of "female hysteria." I find that stereotype repugnant, of course, but if you are a woman, it's important to understand that most people, particularly men, may be uncomfortable in allowing you to express your anger. Communication, either with your grief partner or within the context of grief therapy, as well as writing about your feelings in your grief journal, enables you to deal more positively with this complex emotion. Meditation, yoga, and other forms of exercise are helpful in dealing with many of the physical symptoms associated with anger. Most important, avoiding people who may incite you to anger is the strongest proactive step you can take to avoid unnecessary tangles.

Finally, although much of this chapter has been devoted to ways in which surviving siblings can reduce or avoid anger, please understand that anger is a normal, healthy emotion with regard to the loss of a loved one. You are entitled to feel anger at the injustice of your brother's or sister's death, and feelings of anger connected to your sibling's death will probably surface every now and then for the rest of your life. My hope, however, is that you express your anger in healthy and appropriate ways that both validate your feelings and maintain your dignity.

6

GUILT, REGRET, CONFLICTS

Shoulda, Coulda, Woulda

*Out beyond the ideas of wrongdoing and rightdoing,
there is a field.
I'll meet you there.*

—RUMI

I SIT beside my mother and watch as she slowly turns the pages of the tattered old photo album and feel like I'm five again, snuggling next to Mommy as she reads from a children's book. But this isn't a children's book, and I'm too old for snuggling. With each turn of page, the photographs tell the story of our family. I watch as my childhood parades past; on one page, I'm a fat, smiling infant, on the next I'm a five year-old with tiny, white Chiclet teeth. In a few short pages, I grow up before my eyes: a gawky teenager with Bozo hair and metal braces; a high school senior wearing a ridiculous hat I *thought* looked cool; a young college graduate in dark glasses; a bride; and, finally, a young mother, swimming with my children in my parents' backyard pool.

My mother's life, too, unfolds: at first, a shy young mother with two little children, and then a harried, tired-looking version of the younger model, dogged by a pack of five. Toward the end of the album, a more relaxed, older version emerges, smiling as she proudly cradles her newest grandbaby.

"You look lovely in this one," she says quietly, admiring me in a yellow chiffon prom gown she talked me into wearing (and which I hated). "Ah, this one is good," she says of the photo of my sister Tracy and her new baby. On the next page, she stops and admires a photo of her five children, gathered around a birthday cake. She lingers for a moment, lovingly moving her fingertips across the image. It's the first time either of us has looked at photographs that include my brother since his death several months ago. My head is buzzing, and I have a lump in my throat the size of a tennis ball.

The lump started on the third page with an old black-and-white photograph of my brother at age eight. He stood in the center of the photograph, smiling on command, gapped front teeth and a whiffle haircut, flanked by two younger sisters with messed-up hair. A third, older, sister reads on the couch, ignoring the photographer. "You kids look like hobos in those dumpy play clothes," my mother would always say with a chuckle whenever she'd look at that particular picture—and we'd all howl with laughter. But this time, she just touches the face of her boy and wipes the tears from her eyes with the balled-up Kleenex she keeps in her fist.

Halfway through the album is a photograph of my brother, then twelve, and his friend David after a snowstorm. In the picture, both boys heft a brick of snow on one shoulder; they'd spent the day fashioning an impressive igloo out of snow blocks. As I study the photograph, I suddenly remember details about the day it was taken.

I see my brother and his childhood friend crouched behind the old Plymouth station wagon in our driveway, waiting for an unsuspecting victim to pass. As fate would have it, that victim was me. Coming home from a morning of sledding, I drag my battered old sled behind me, unaware of the impending attack. I'm seven. As I approach the driveway, concentrating on keeping my footing on the icy hill, David and my brother hurl snowballs at me from behind the parked car. They'd spent nearly an hour amassing their arsenal and both have exceedingly good aim.

It takes me a minute to figure out the source of the assault, but I when hear my brother's distinctive Woody Woodpecker laughter coming from behind the car, I know instantly the identity of my assailants—well, at least one of them. As I scramble to find cover behind a clump of bushes, I slip and fall face first into a mound of ice-encrusted snow. I lift my head and see a tiny smear of blood; I move my tongue to my lower lip and taste salt.

Of course, I start to cry. I try to get up to show my brother my split lip, but the attack intensifies. Snowballs pummel my thick green parka, and I cover my face and broken lip with my mittens. I crawl on my stomach to the twisted juniper bush, crying and yelling for them to stop.

As they reload, I decide to make a run for the kitchen door. I pull myself to an indignant standing position, glare in the direction of the old Plymouth, and scream, "I hate you, you big, fat creep!"

Just at that moment, two stocking-capped twelve-year-olds emerge from around the car, ammunition in hand, smiling. David hits me in the head with a frozen chunk, and I cry harder. My brother, about to join in, stops when he see my bloody lip. He drops his snowball to the ground and runs to me, slipping and sliding, his face a mixture of concern and fear. "Wait'll I tell Mom what you did!" I threaten through tears. He yells over his shoulder to David, "Cut it out! She's hurt!" David quickly retreats, shamefaced, behind the Plymouth. My brother crunches up in front of me and pulls off his glove. Taking my face into his hand he examines my war wound. I cry extra hard now for emphasis. "It's all right," he tells me. "You'll live."

He puts his arm around my shoulder and walks me into the house. My mother rushes over when she sees the blood and the theatrical tears. "How did this happen?" she asks, dabbing my chin with a dishtowel. My brother looks guiltily down at his Army Ranger boots. "Well?" she demands. "How did this happen?" I look over at my big brother, and he lifts his gaze, blue eyes pleading. I hesitate. I'm so angry that I feel like kicking him, but I can't bring myself to rat on him.

"I was running and I fell down," I tell my mother. She looks suspicious, but accepts the answer. "Go wash your face," she says and returns to her chores. My brother sighs with relief and gives my arm a little punch as he races out the back door to continue work on his igloo. I stand in wet clothes, alone in the kitchen, tears running down my cheeks. Not because of my fat lip, but because I just remembered I told the person I most adore that I hated him. And I also called him a big, fat creep.

After Jim's [age 54] accident, and particularly after his death six weeks later, I found myself sorting through old memories and recalling our childhood relationship. We grew up in a somewhat dysfunctional family and were not close until well into adulthood. I actively disliked him when he was small and remember teasing him until he cried and abusing him in various other childish ways. I had one memory of deliberately ignoring him one time at school, when he was injured on the playground. It turned out that he had broken a bone in his foot. Now I feel very remorseful about my overall attitude toward him in childhood. I wish that I could have been more loving, more of a sister to him. I suspect that this sort of thinking is not unusual in the bereaved.

—JANET, 57

Janet poignantly describes the type of sibling guilt we often carry from childhood into adulthood. In fact, because we've known our siblings all our lives, we may have an excessive amount of guilt baggage: guilt from our childhood, guilt from the teenage years, guilt from the young adult years (when we were off "finding ourselves" and decided that our family was no longer good enough for us), and, if we're lucky, guilt about things we do or say to our brothers and sisters in midlife and on into the twilight years.

Regret and guilt often plague bereaved siblings as we reflect back to what we should have, could have, or would have done, *if we had only known.* We would have called our sibling more often, been a better brother or sister, gotten together more, and helped them more with their problems; and we certainly would have told our brother or sister how much they meant to us, if only we had known.

My sister, Debra [age 44], had Huntington's disease, a fatal ill-ness that would have taken her life within the next decade, after first destroying most of her ability to function. I did not want to see my sister deteriorate to a near-vegetative state, but she ended up dying in a car accident, so I have regrets and guilt of a differ-ent sort. I wish that I could have had just a little more time with my sister; I would have done more to make her remaining time happy and special. I tell myself that I would have had infinite patience with her disease, which made her at times difficult to deal with. I hate myself, now, for all of those phone calls I cut short or did not return during that last year of her life and for the long blocks of time that passed between our visits.

—TRACY, 41

Sometimes these regrets and feelings of remorse are legiti-mate; that is, perhaps we had been unkind to our brother or sister prior to his or her death. But, more often than not, guilt and re-gret are our own private form of self-flagellation—punishment we neither earned nor deserve. For example, many surviving sib-lings, like Sherry, punish themselves for not being superhuman enough to prevent their sibling's death in the first place.

Why didn't I do more to help Jimmy [age 39]? How could his addiction be so life threatening and I didn't know about it? I was his big sister. I should have protected him as I always did when we were growing up. —SHERRY, 47

Sherry's reaction is typical of eldest siblings, the self-appointed guardians of the flock. When a younger sibling dies, they often assume a level of responsibility for their brother's or sister's death that we middle and youngest children can't under-stand. But guilt and remorse are often based more on conditioning than on fact. In Sherry's case, for instance, anyone who has ever grown up with a sibling who's had addiction problems knows there's usually not much anyone in the family can do to remedy the situation; addicts need professional help. Still, as the oldest child in her family, Sherry felt she should have been able to protect her little brother and is overcome with guilt and regret for not being able to do so. Of course, feeling responsibility for a sibling's death is not limited to the eldest in the family, as B. G. points out.

I felt a certain amount of responsibility/guilt about my brother's death because I knew of his pain, and I wished that he had been able to share it more openly with me, as I had with him. His note to me, mailed on the day of his death, was not angry or manipulative. He asked for my understanding and acceptance of his decision to end his life, closing with the phrase, "When you read this, I will at last be at peace." I trust that this is the case. Twenty-one years later, I still miss and love him.

—B. G., 49

I don't think any of us has lived through grief without at least a few regrets or feelings of remorse. One of the more maddening aspects of grief is the time we spend reviewing the details of our relationship with our brother or sister. In most cases, we come up with a laundry list of deficiencies that all lead to the same conclusion: I wasn't a good enough brother or sister to my sibling. After all, it's much easier to kick ourselves around when we feel terrible, anyway.

I had many guilty feelings: the fact that I hadn't seen Dana [age 21] for two months; that when I saw her for the last time, I did not tell her that I loved her; that I didn't hug her good-bye; that I was not with her when she died; that I may have contributed to her unhappiness. All these things turned over and over in my mind. How could I have done this thing or that thing? Even now, once in a while, a guilt twinge hits me like a rock and I feel terrible.
—RONNA, 34

In families, particularly large families, alliances form. I'm not sure why some siblings click and others don't; I only know that in my own family, even though I love all of my sisters fiercely, I related better to my brother than to any of them. I never had a major disagreement with my brother, although I can't make a similar claim about my sisters. This is not to say that I don't regret some of the things I said or did with regard to my brother, because I do. I regret not visiting him more; I regret putting him in the middle of squabbles between my mother and me; but most of all, I regret leaving him while he was dying.

I remember talking to my brother in the hospital shortly before he died. I told him that I didn't know how to go on living in a world that didn't include him; it seemed too strange and alien even to contemplate. I told him that I had never closed my eyes and gone to sleep without remembering him in my prayers, the prayers we both learned and recited together as children: "Now I lay me down to sleep,/pray the Lord my soul to keep./Guide me safely through the night,/and wake me in the morning light." (My mother changed this last line for us, thinking the more traditional, "If I should die before I wake, I pray the Lord my soul to take" too morbid.) I still ended with, "God bless Mom and Pop and Linda, Robin, VJay and Tracy." In later years, my husband and children had been appended to the litany. How could I possibly lay my head on my pillow at night, much less recite that prayer, knowing that my brother was no longer a part of this world? It was utterly inconceivable to me that life would actually continue without him. I remember feeling cold and very afraid. The world, as I had always known it, was slowly slipping away, and I was completely powerless to stop it. And so I did what any good coward does—I headed for the hills.

Just moments before my brother slipped into a coma, I held his hand and said good-bye, and then, unlike other family members who remained with him until he took his final breath, I left. To this day, this remains the single biggest regret of my life.

It was very painful for our whole family that no one was at the hospital with Stefani [age 25] when she died. She was there alone, and since she was not carrying identification, no one there even knew her name. It was especially painful for me because I had driven within 150 yards of the accident scene the night before, on my way to a Neighborhood Watch meeting. I saw an ambulance and police officers directing traffic, but I went on to my meeting. I wish I could have been with Stefani to hold her hand on the way to the hospital. I know it would not have prevented her death, but it made her death even more sad because she spent the last hours of her life alone, without anyone there to comfort her.

—DEAN, 30

I recently discussed my feelings of regret with my good friend Nancy R. "I can't believe you feel guilty about leaving your brother," she said. "Surely you must know, at least intellectually, that your brother would never hold such a thing against you—that he would understand and accept your decision to go simply because he loved you so much."

"Yes," I tell her, "I know he understands—but I also know that he never would have left *me*."

I try to explain to Nancy that these feelings, irrational though they may seem to nongrievers, are all part of the package of grief—and that this is why grief is unlike anything else we've ever experienced and why it's so hard.

For instance, I can read Dean's story and think, "How could you have known the person being treated by the paramedics was your own sister? You shouldn't feel guilty about something that was totally out of your control." But I know that no matter how many people tell Dean such things, he will always regret not walking those 150 yards across the street to where his sister lay dying.

But grief, of course, can't be reduced to a mere intellectual exercise. Nothing illustrates this point better than the experience of *survivor guilt*. Survivor guilt is when a sibling expresses feelings of guilt or regret at being alive while his or her brother or sister has died. Some surviving siblings believe that fate missed her mark and took the wrong sibling by mistake. Many even feel as if their dead sibling's life was somehow more worthy or more valuable than their own.

> *I was angry at God for allowing this happen to Patsy [age 45]. Why not me? My life didn't amount to anything.*
> —KATHY-ANNE, 53

> *I remember that I did wish it had been me instead of Lori [age 31]. She was a perfect mother, and I felt so useless. I felt that she was needed on this earth more than I.* —DEBBIE, 37

Another issue that can trigger feelings of survivor guilt is money. In many cases, particularly when there are only two children in the family and both parents are deceased, surviving siblings are often the executor and the beneficiary of the deceased sibling's estate. This may mean you receive some form of monetary gain, including cash, stocks, bonds, or other valuables, upon your sibling's death.

> *I am the administrator of Paul's [age 48] estate because our father suffers from Alzheimer's and Parkinson's. I've been experiencing sorrow and guilt because I will benefit financially from his death.* —L. B., 55

The subsequent guilt that accompanies a financial gain stipulated in our brother's or sister's will only serves to compound our feelings of remorse. Further, many surviving siblings experience intense feelings of survivor guilt triggered by what amounts to an improved quality of life that has been made possible only by a sibling's demise.

I profited enormously from my brother's death. Before, I was liv-
ing in a tiny apartment in a small town, working hard at a low-
paying, high-stress job that I disliked, and struggling to make
ends meet. I had little in the way of a social or recreational life.
I didn't have the energy. Now I'm retired at 57, living in a
beautiful home high on a hill overlooking San Francisco Bay,
and enjoying the attentions of a number of warm and supportive
people (my brother's friends) who stay in touch with me, offer
their help, and invite me to do things and go places with them. I
am overwhelmed with feelings of gratitude and feelings of guilt.
Sometimes, when the guilt becomes unmanageable, I remind
myself, in just these words: I did not kill my brother.

—JANET, 57

We often feel guilty accepting the money in the first place, almost as if the very act of accepting funds somehow indicates that
we're attaching a monetary value to our brother's or sister's death.
Taking the money often seems *wrong*, like a betrayal. It feels as if
we're somehow reducing our sibling's life to what's left behind.

As executor of Bob's [age 48] estate, I had much to do to settle
his affairs. This gave me a feeling of usefulness, but it also made
me feel at times that I was "disposing" of him as I sold his prop-
erties and other assets. —SUNNY, 75

Even though others may try to convince us that our brother
or sister would want us to have a better life and that we should
therefore consider the money a gift, it still feels like a compensa-
tion of sorts for our loss. Andrea, whose brother Ed was killed
during the attack on the Pentagon on September 11, 2001, captures these feelings best.

Some people asked: "How much money do you think your family
will get out of this? How are you going to spend it? Your brother

would want you to celebrate, don't you think?" My parents, my sister, our extended family, and I didn't care about the money. We would have given it ALL back just to have Ed [age 26] here. —ANDREA, 31

Finally, the question of what to do with the money often becomes a huge issue. Some surviving siblings can't bear to spend the money, while others feel the need to spend it in some meaningful way.

I had a financial gain due to my sister's death and have still not been able to touch this money. I want very much to use it for something highly beneficial to humanity and have not been able to choose. —ELISE, 36

Surviving siblings may feel guilt over childhood issues, for not preventing a brother's or sister's death, for being alive while a sibling has died, or for benefiting financially from his or her death. All of these forms of guilt are difficult to bear. But for most siblings, what we regret most are the simple things: not having the chance to say good-bye; failing to tell our sibling how much we'd miss him or her; missing the opportunity to apologize for any wrong we may have caused; forgetting to say "I love you" just one more time.

I wish that I had told Sarah [age 36] how much I would miss her. My parents did not want to upset Sarah, so we never talked about dying. —PAULA, 42

• • •

Conflicts, disagreements, and rivalries are inevitable aspects of family life and of life in general. Of course, one of the most defining features of the sibling relationship is the lifelong competition we share with our sisters and brothers, beginning with the competition for our parents' affection and approval. Sibling rivalry is both commonplace and distinctive: commonplace in that nearly all brothers and sisters display some degree of rivalry at one time or another, and distinctive in that this particular type of lifelong competition is usually absent in other relationships.

> *Most of our lives, Andy [age 25] and I were in conflict. His life was based on alcohol, drugs, and rock music. I was basically a "good girl." We really antagonized each other while we lived at home. About a year before he died, he started trying to get help and entered rehab. At that time, we started developing a friendship. I came to appreciate the good qualities in him and to really care what happened to him. The last time I saw him was at Christmastime. We had both gone home to stay with our mom for a few days. Andy and I played board games and cards, built fires, talked, played with our younger brother (who was eleven years old at the time). I remember thinking how great it was to have a friendship with my brother. Before I left for the five-hundred-mile trip home, I hugged Andy and said, jokingly, "It's been nice seeing you, but I could never live with you again!" Those were the last words I ever said to him.*
>
> —LISA-MARIE, 34

Lisa-Marie and Andy eventually grew beyond the conflicts of their shared past and eased into a more mature, comfortable relationship that seemed to work well for both of them. This kind of relationship metamorphosis is rare outside of families, but it is often the hallmark of the adult sibling relationship.

Many sibling relationships, however, bear the scars of childhood pain—scars that may interfere with attempts at reconciliation in later years. For instance, some siblings are unable to shake off their old roles from childhood and fall immediately into them once they're in the company of their brothers and sisters. Perhaps you've tried to have a mature relationship with your sibling, only to find that neither of you was able to work through the difficulties from your childhood. After several failed attempts to forge an adult relationship with your brother or sister, maybe you just gave up and accepted the fact that you and your sibling would always be estranged. Or perhaps you harbored secret hopes of an eventual reconciliation at some future date, thinking you had all the time in the world to work things out. Naturally, when a brother or sister with whom you've had a somewhat strained relationship passes away, the subsequent guilt can certainly complicate mourning.

> *I felt guilt that I had not tried to reach out more to Marshall [age 46], but it was always so hard between us—unresolved sibling rivalry and the fact that we were so different. But no one could tell him anything, least of all me, the younger brother who had done all of the "right" things and to whom he had never been close. He had always suffered from low self-esteem, I think, and his deterioration and death were all part of that scenario.*
>
> —FRANK, 52

The common history we share with our brothers and sisters spans a lifetime and is unlike any other relationship we will ever experience. Whether your relationship with your brother or sister was smooth and easy, fraught with conflict, or somewhere in between, your sibling relationship has contributed, in many ways, to the person you are today.

· · ·

Imagine this: You and your sister have always had a mercurial relationship. As children, you rarely got along, and as adolescents, you barely spoke to each other. As you both grew and matured into adulthood, each marrying and starting a family, your relationship slowly transformed from one riddled with conflict into a loving, supportive friendship. Except for one thing. You hate your sister's husband.

Now, imagine your sister dies.

Not only must you deal with the death of your sister, but now, in order to spend time with your nieces and nephews, you must cultivate a relationship with your sister's husband, who probably feels as negatively toward you as you do toward him. Many surviving siblings actually lose touch with their nieces and nephews after their brother or sister dies, particularly if their sibling's spouse remarries. Of course, the remarriage itself presents a variety of new obstacles for the family of the deceased sibling, especially if the remarriage occurs soon after the sibling's death.

> *My brother and his wife were having problems prior to his death. The day before he was to be buried, she asked me how long I thought it should take before my family would accept her dating again. Two months later, she had a man move in with her, and seven months after Bob's [age 33] death, she became pregnant. Our family has never been the same.* —TAMI, 26

Conflicts with a brother's or sister's other family (your sibling's spouse/partner, children, or assorted in-laws) are oftentimes more troublesome than the conflicts you may have within your family of origin. Because your sibling's other family is more a part of your sibling's life rather than your own, it's natural to feel a little discomfort dealing with people you probably don't know very well.

Issues ranging from funeral arrangements, wills, and financial matters to your brother's or sister's children and possibly the eventual remarriage of your sibling's spouse often result in bitter feuds, even litigation. These conflicts can lead to a permanent rift, which, of course, compounds your grief, particularly when your nieces and nephews are involved. In Rosemary's case, the conflicts with her sister-in-law following her brother's death were especially volatile.

A few months after Sean's [age 43] death, his widow allowed her twenty-eight-year-old handyman to move in with her and the six children. She spent the $600,000 life insurance on fancy vacations, clothes, and cars. One day, she showed my parents a metal box supposedly containing Sean's ashes. My parents were very upset because they were under the impression that his ashes had been scattered in Virginia (where he died). They wanted to put the ashes in the family plot, and we planned a ceremony for the first anniversary of Sean's death. The day before the ceremony, Sean's widow called and told us that she had decided not to give us the ashes after all. I flew into a rage and stormed into her house screaming, "I want my brother's ashes!" The police were called, and I was sent home. Surprisingly, later that evening, Sean's widow called and said she'd have the ashes at the cemetery as planned. We had the ceremony and interred the ashes. Sean's widow hugged me and said, "You know, I really do love you." A few months later, we found out from my brother's children that the ashes weren't really Sean's remains at all, but sand from a nearby field. —ROSEMARY, 51

Thankfully, most conflicts rarely escalate to the level Rosemary describes, but even minor clashes can make what is already an emotionally draining period in your life even worse.

Although guilt, regret, and conflicts are normal aspects of bereavement, they can be powerfully destructive. We need to learn ways to deal with the various issues that derail us from establishing a healthy relationship with our brother or sister, despite the fact that he or she is no longer alive. In doing this, we begin the process of integrating our loss into our life in a healing and meaningful way.

WHAT HELPS

What if your relationship with your sibling was stormy and marked with conflict at the time of his or her death? What if you always believed you and your sibling would somehow reconcile over time, only to find that time had run out? How can you begin to heal from your loss when you're consumed with guilt for not being a more loving brother or sister? And what about your brother's or sister's other family? How do you deal with *them*?

What follows are several suggestions that might help you to better deal with issues of guilt, regret, and conflict.

Let's begin with the relationship between you and your sibling. If you and your brother or sister had a turbulent history, marred with unresolved problems that are now causing you a great deal of guilt and regret, you might consider writing a letter to your sibling as a way of letting go of these feelings. This is an exercise often used in therapy and most find it extremely helpful. There are a variety of techniques and styles you can employ to write such a letter, but I think it's best simply to write from the heart. Ask yourself: If I had the chance to sit down with my brother or sister and talk about the pain between us, what would I say? Don't pay any attention to grammar, style, or length. Just write what you feel.

You may decide to do this exercise and keep your letter to yourself, or you might consider reading your letter aloud to your grief partner or a trusted friend. Reading the letter aloud often has a cathartic effect, as Jan describes.

After I finished attending the Grief Recovery support group (offered by a funeral home in our area), I could talk about my brothers' [Eddie, age 46; Dennis, age 34; and Dwayne, age 36] deaths without crying. Our last assignment was to write a letter to our deceased loved ones and then read them. It was a gut-

wrenching experience, but I felt as if a ton had been lifted from
my shoulders.   —JAN, 56

Jan's letter was written in the context of a sibling survivor
group she attended after losing three of her siblings in the course
of only two years. With so much grief in such a short period of
time, Jan was wise to participate in a survivors' group. In fact,
most siblings can benefit greatly from the experience of such
groups. There's healing in simply sharing your feelings with others who truly understand your pain because they're experiencing
something similar. Although I'll discuss survivors' groups and
individual therapy in more detail in chapter 7, it's important to
remember that there are some issues you may not be able to handle on your own. If you find you just can't seem to focus on anything other than your guilt and regret, this is an indication that
the problem is bigger than you and that it's probably time to seek
professional help.

For most of us, however, guilt and regret are basically
aspects of the greater complex of grief emotions. With this in
mind, many survivors choose not to focus on guilt or conflict
issues at all, but on the positive side of their sibling relationship.
Chances are that you've probably already exhausted yourself
lamenting over problems that, given the fact that your sibling is
no longer alive, will never be resolved. Sadly, there's very little
you can do to change things now. After all, psychologists often
remind us that although we can't change the past, we *can* change
our reactions to it. Hence, you might begin by looking back over
your sibling's life and trying to recall the loving, affirming, positive aspects of the relationship you shared. The intention here is
to shift your focus to the good times, the happy memories, and
say good-bye to the guilt that's making you miserable.

You can begin this process by simply recalling times when
you and your sibling shared special moments. These may be
childhood memories or more recent memories. Maybe you can

recall certain meaningful conversations or times when you just plain had fun. For example, one of my fondest memories is the day I cajoled all of my adult siblings into going trail-riding with me. I was the only person in the group who knew how to ride a horse, and after some initial protests, I finally convinced the more reticent siblings that we'd have a good time. And we did. In fact, I'll never forget my brother, who was among the last of the siblings to arrive at the farm, mounted on a mule (by the time he arrived, all of the horses had been taken), laughing and bouncing around in his saddle as the mule ignored his feeble tug on the reins and ran off in a totally different direction.

We took photographs of that day, and looking at them now still makes me laugh out loud. If you're having difficulty in recalling better times, spend a few hours looking through old photo albums. This activity is certain to trigger memories of better times.

> *I think of the things Paul [age 48] said to me over the last couple of years during phone conversations and the good times we shared when we were a lot younger and still living at home with the folks, and I take much comfort in those things.*
>
> —L. B., 55

Replacing painful memories that conjure feelings of guilt and regret with happier memories is not an easy process; it's often difficult to let go of the guilt and put the arguments and conflicts behind us. And, of course, this change in perspective is not likely to happen overnight. One of the ways you can help yourself to learn to focus on the positive aspects of your sibling relationship is to create some sort of enduring memorial. For example, making something as simple as a photographic collage of you and your sibling can serve to remind you of the happier times you shared. Or you might consider creating a sibling storybook—the story of you and your brother or sister, a history of sorts that you can share with others. Or instead of writing a sibling history, you might choose to write about one particularly funny incident that highlights something special about your relationship. Photographs and other keepsakes can help illustrate your story; or, if you're not much of a writer, let the photographs and keepsakes tell the entire story. Be sure to give your book a meaningful title—something that captures the essence of your relationship with your brother or sister.

You can make your storybook using a scrapbook, a fabric-covered journal, or any other blank, prefabricated book. Or you might want to design your book using your computer and then have it professionally bound and laminated. Do whatever your creative talents allow, but be sure the book tells your story, in your words. Here, Heidi discusses the sibling story she and her brother wrote prior to his death. The book is, I'm sure, a great source of comfort to her now that Michael is gone.

Michael [age 34] and I wrote our story together, mainly because so little was available about personal struggles of catastrophic illnesses and so little available on the strength of sibling relationships. The writing was one of the most precious things we ever shared together. The love we expressed helped both of us transform and transcend the pain of our circumstance. The title is "Tapestry of Love: A Brother, a Sister, and an Odyssey Through Cancer."

—HEIDI, 34

Another way to shift your focus away from the hurt caused by guilt and regret is to create a memory quilt. There are a variety of approaches you can take in constructing the memory quilt, but it should not be merely a display item (like the AIDS quilt). The intention here is to literally wrap yourself in memories. If possible, the quilt should be constructed of materials belonging both to you and your brother or sister. The quilt should be small, no bigger than four by six feet, and each square should tell a story, either through the fabric used or through images (including photographs—yes, there's actually a way to transfer photographs to fabric!) that hold special meaning.

There are several excellent resources that can help you get started, including websites from which you can both receive instruction and purchase supplies (see "Chapter Resources" in the appendix).

If you're not interested in creating a collage, writing a letter, writing a sibling storybook, or putting together a memory quilt, I have one final suggestion that has helped me: have a healing ceremony. A healing ceremony is a ritual that can help you let go of your guilt and regret of the past; it can be a religious ritual or strictly secular. The healing ceremony in which I participated was nondenominational, but there are certain religions that have prescribed healing rituals.

My healing ceremony included only myself and two other women, one of whom was a surviving sibling, but you can invite anyone you'd like, perhaps making it a family affair or something you do among a few trusted friends. Although healing rituals vary, we found comfort in listening to uplifting music, reading from the psalms, and participating in a hand-washing ceremony. The hand-washing ceremony was particularly meaningful: One person pours water over your hands while another "washes" away your guilt and regret. As your hands are being washed, you may talk about your guilt and regrets or simply reflect upon them in silence. It's important to surrender to the person washing your hands, allowing her to offer you condolence and support. The water from your hand washing is gathered into a vial, which you then empty into the sea. This symbolic action represents the letting go of your guilt and regrets.

The intentions behind the collage, the sibling letter, the memorial storybook, the quilt, and the healing ceremony are similar: These are all actions that can help liberate you from the guilt and regret that can increase the pain of your loss and instead help you to recall the good times you shared with your sibling. Whenever possible, where guilt and regret are concerned, it's best to just let them go.

> *I finally let go of the guilt I had for not being a better sibling and friend to James [age 29] around the time I began to accept his death.* —NADINE, 41

. . .

Now, how do you deal with your sibling's other family? Specifically, how can surviving siblings work though conflicts and disagreements with those pesky relatives who are part of your brother's or sister's family? Obviously, not all surviving siblings encounter obstacles and conflicts in dealing with their sibling's in-laws. In fact, a sibling's other family sometimes can provide healing and comfort in ways your family of origin can't. Moreover, many survivors maintain a close relationship with their sibling's spouse or partner, as Jan's family did.

> *My sister-in-law remarried a super guy who is very good to my niece and nephew. He's like one of the family and comes to family gatherings, sometimes even bringing his mother along. She's a very nice lady, and we're glad to have them both. I think it's better when you can see others eventually going on with life and not feeling such extreme sadness.* —JAN, 56

But what if the opposite is true? What if the actions of your brother's or sister's other family, particularly his or her spouse, are causing you more heartache during a time when you've already had your fill of sorrow?

> *Less than a year after Nancy [age 40] died, her husband, who has not remarried, asked my other sister to baby-sit for him because he had a date. This led to an ugly spat between Nancy's*

husband and my family. There continue to be problems between Nancy's husband (and Nancy's mother-in-law, who we felt was unsupportive during Nancy's illness) and my family. It makes me sad, all of this bitterness, because not only does it affect Nancy's son in a negative way, but it is also the last thing Nancy would have wanted after her death. She always tried to keep things together while she was alive and tried to keep harmony between the two families; all that has come apart since she died.

—J. ELIZABETH, 31

It can be painful to see our sibling's spouse move on with his or her life while our brother or sister cannot. Intellectually, we understand that as sad as we may feel, life does goes on. Still, most of us can sympathize with Elizabeth. Although her brother-in-law was obviously ready to move on, one must question his judgment in asking his dead wife's sister to baby-sit while he goes out on a date. Yet Elizabeth's family is caught in a very precarious trap: In order to continue maintaining a connection with Nancy's child, they must, in essence, make nice with Nancy's husband. If a falling-out were to occur, Nancy's family would suffer yet another loss: the loss of visitation with the one remaining link to Nancy—her son.

My advice in dealing with your brother's or sister's other family is to first try to avoid conflicts whenever possible. If you anticipate a battle, be certain that you're mentally prepared—or at least as prepared as you can be, under the circumstances. If you suspect a confrontation may result from a meeting with your sibling's other family, review the details of the situation with your grief partner, including *your* desired resolution, and then include your grief partner when you meet with the "opposition." Having a calm voice of reason on your side can make all the difference. And in cases where a volatile relationship has already been established, it's best to try to keep meetings and conversations brief and to the point.

Although some issues are more complex than others, compromise whenever possible. Few people are willing simply to abandon their position, but most are willing to meet you halfway. Decide what you're able to live with, and then be willing to bend a little, if required. This can be difficult, of course, especially when conflicts arise over such things as money.

> *Because Pat [age 48] was killed in a head-on train accident caused by a dispatcher, who put two trains on the same track, there was settlement money for his children. The battle over the money sickened me. It was as though they lost all sight of the loss of my brother.*
> —LINDA, 51

Finally, it's important to make a distinction between the typical family quarrels that can be resolved with sincere, open dialogue and the more severe, irreconcilable disputes that can be so damaging. In cases where neither side is able to reach an agreement, or if there's a great deal of hostility on both sides (as in Rosemary's story on page 144), it's a good idea to involve a third-party mediator to help settle disagreements. This person should be an individual agreed upon by both parties; you might, for example, ask a mutual family friend or a clergyperson, or engage the services of a professional mediator. The bigger the conflict, the more important it is to have an unbiased arbitrator involved in helping each side come to a peaceful resolution.

Remember, too, that you're not yourself right now; you're working through your own grief and dealing with the fallout of this terrible trauma. Keep this in mind and make sure you don't minimize your grief in deference to your sibling's other family. For example, you may feel at a disadvantage in dealing with your sibling's wife because you perceive her loss as greater than your own. You might therefore back down from an important issue simply because your sibling's spouse is "the widow" and you're "just a sibling." If you feel strongly about certain issues, you have every right to be heard. After all, your loss is every bit as legitimate, even if others fail to acknowledge it.

Guilt, regret, and conflicts complicate mourning by deflecting the energy we need to deal with our loss to a negative focus on a past we're powerless to change. We need to free ourselves from the stranglehold of guilt and regret through constructive activities that shift our focus to the more positive aspects of our sibling relationship. In the same way, avoiding, minimizing, or defusing conflicts whenever possible helps us to move forward in our journey of grief.

7

DEPRESSION

How Low Can You Go?

To be creatures who love, we must be creatures who can despair at what we lose, and depression is the mechanism of that despair.

—ANDREW SOLOMON

M Y HUSBAND's birthday is just days away and the only thing left to buy is the card. All I want is a simple card with a heartfelt, loving message, but I'm having a difficult time finding one among the thousands of cards in the Hallmark store. The salesclerk, a tiny woman with rimless glasses, seems annoyed to have a lone customer frustrating her efforts to close at precisely 9:00 and makes a big show of locking one of the doors and noisily counting out change in the register. I get the hint, but I refuse to be bullied into buying a card I don't really want. After all, it's my husband's fortieth birthday; the card has to be just right.

As I move further down the aisle, reading and replacing the silly and overly sentimental cards, I accidentally pick up a birthday card that reads, "For my brother, on his special day." I freeze for a moment, feeling both startled and then strangely guilty, as if I've just been caught taking something that doesn't belong to me. I quickly return the brother card to its rightful place and steal a glance at the salesclerk, wondering if she saw me meddling in the brother-card section, where I no longer belong. I imagine her racing down the aisle, arms waving, ordering me out of the store. "Just what do you think you're doing?" she'd yell. "That section is for people who have brothers! Can't you read the sign?"

Then she'd point to the door. "Get out!" she'd say, trying to keep her voice under control. "And stay away from those brother cards! Everyone knows you don't even *have* a brother anymore."

I snap out of my ridiculous fantasy only to realize there are tears running down my cheeks. As I frantically search my pockets and purse for a tissue, the salesclerk appears from nowhere and matter-of-factly hands me a Kleenex. She smiles knowingly, as if this sort of thing happens all the time in her store. "Cry all you want, honey," she says as she touches a hand to my shoulder. "There's no one else in the store." Compassion, it seems, comes in many forms.

After a few minutes, I blow my nose, thank the saleslady for her kindness, and leave the store for the safety of my car. As I make the short drive home, I feel it coming—the familiar dark mood that visits me with great frequency these days. It hums around me at first, assessing my defenses—and then, like ink on blotter, it spreads quickly, spilling into my consciousness, until I'm enveloped in its immutable blackness.

· · ·

In my grief journal, I write, "I feel as if I'm moving in slow-motion. I'm forgetful and short-tempered and everything seems meaningless; work, cleaning the house, shuttling the kids from one event to the next—it all seems so pointless. Why bother? I think I'm depressed." Although I use the word *depressed* to describe the awful, hopeless feeling I'm experiencing, I'm not quite sure if what I'm feeling is technically depression—at least, not in the clinical sense. Isn't it normal, after all, to feel depressed when someone you've loved all your life has died?

> *Stefani's [age 25] birthday came five months after her death, and Christmas came a month after that. About a month later, I realized how depressed I had become. Never having really experienced depression before, I didn't recognize it when it hit me. The most insidious part of it was that at first I couldn't identify Stefani's death as being the underlying cause of how terrible I felt. Prior to Stefani's death, I had always been self-confident, ambitious, and relatively happy. But in the depths of depression, every aspect of my life was inundated with sadness, despair, and feelings of*

inadequacy and self-doubt. Friends and family asked me if I was feeling bad because of Stefani's death, and I thought, "Yes, but everything else in my life sucks, too."　　　—DEAN, 30

By now, I've read scores of grief books, and I know that most grieving people experience some form of depression following the death of a sibling, but my experience of depression doesn't seem to fit the mold. Yes, I feel miserable and desolate sometimes, but these feelings can best be described as sudden and transient, usually triggered by some seemingly innocuous event, like turning the calendar to a new month or hearing a particular song on the radio. I'm fine one moment and tumbling headlong into despair the next. There are days when the depression is so bad that it takes every ounce of strength just to get out of bed and go to work. And, despite my busy and active life, I'm often lonely. I worry that I've become a burden to my husband, children, and friends, so I keep to myself when I'm feeling down—but this only contributes to my loneliness.

Edna St. Vincent Millay wrote, "The presence of that absence is everywhere." And it *is*. My brother's palpable absence lingers on the edge of every thought, every feeling, every action; it's always *there*. In many ways, the depression is always there, too, hovering along the sidelines. The only thing that keeps it at bay is sheer will, and even that often fails me.

My depression is still present. I consider it my deep, introspective, immovable, great, hunched-over companion.

　　　—ELISE, 36

But there are also good days now. Minutes and hours pass without a shadow of sadness, and sometimes I even forget I'm still mourning. These moments of joy are always tempered, however, by the now-familiar longing that stifles genuine contentment.

Still, I wonder: Is this *depression* or just normal grief? In trying to figure out whether I'm actually depressed, I need to understand what depression is and how it pertains to grief. I learn that depression is a serious health condition that presently affects about 17.6 million people in the United States each year. If you've never experienced depression, however, it's often difficult to recognize the symptoms. According to the National Institute of Mental Health's Depression Awareness, Recognition, and Treatment program, these symptoms typically include a persistent sad or empty-feeling mood; loss of interest or pleasure in doing ordinary things, even things you normally love to do; low energy or fatigue; sleep problems (sleeping too little or too much); eating problems (including weight gain or loss); problems in concentrating (including memory problems) and making decisions; feelings of guilt, worthlessness, or helplessness; thoughts of death or suicide (including suicide attempts); irritability; excessive crying; and chronic aches and pain that fail to respond to treatment. Most experts agree that if you suffer from five or more of these symptoms for more than two weeks, you should seek professional help.

Is there a difference between clinical depression and the depression associated with the death of a loved one? I find a variety of answers to this question, but the response I find most illuminating comes from Dr. Alan Wolfelt in *Death and Grief: A Guide for Clergy*. Wolfelt makes several possible distinctions between normal grief reactions and clinical depression. First, in normal grief, people usually respond to offers of support and comfort; in clinical depression, these offers of support are often refused. In normal grief, the bereaved are often openly angry; in clinical depression, a person may be irritable and might complain, but does not openly express his or her anger. In normal grief, one relates the depression to his or her loss; in other words, you attribute your depression directly to the death of your brother or sister, whereas in clinical depression, your depression is more generalized and unrelated to one specific event. In normal grief, you're still able to experience moments of enjoyment; if you're suffering from clinical depression, on the other hand, there's a pervasive sense of doom. Finally, in normal grief, you may experience transient physical problems, and you may express feelings of guilt over some specific aspect of your loss; in clinical depression, you're more likely to have chronic physical complaints and a more generalized feeling of guilt.

Although these reactions may be classified as normal responses to the death of a sibling, they must be monitored with great care. It's fairly common to start out with normal grief depression only to have it escalate into a more serious form. If, for example, you're having suicidal thoughts, you're no longer dealing with normal grief depression. Here's a good rule of thumb: If you or those around you are even marginally concerned that your grief has crossed the line from a so-called normal grief response to a more serious form of depression, it's time to find professional help (see "What Helps" at the end of this chapter).

For most surviving siblings, depression is the most long-lasting and certainly the most painful aspect of bereavement.

> *I have been struggling with depression for over a year. I withdrew from friends, work, and everyday activities. It takes every bit of energy I have to keep myself from withdrawing from my children at times. I have been dealing with this in a destructive manner and have to pull myself out of my depression by myself, to keep going. Other people have tried to help me, and while I appreciate it, I know I have to get over this on my own.*
>
> —LAURA, 39

Although Laura is fortunate to have others who are concerned enough to offer her comfort, she still feels she must somehow come to terms with Sarah's death in her own way; ultimately, I think this is true for all of us, whether we seek professional help or not. Laura also points out the tendency most people have to deal with grief in destructive ways. Destructive behaviors can range from diminished interest in one's appearance (or general self-neglect) to the use of alcohol, drugs, and food as coping tools (see chapter 4).

> *It's been four full months since Paula [age 59], a recent divorcée, died without warning in her sleep. All through the dark winter months (in Alaska), I hid in my bed reading novels furiously and hoping that the phone wouldn't ring. I ate terrible things that I feared would kill me: bags of potato chips, ice cream, and cashews. I was just too sad to talk about it, and my husband worked until I was asleep most nights. It was as if he had gotten over losing her quickly, but I couldn't let her go. I still cry some days, two or three times.* —MARTHA, 46

> *Losing Bryan [age 28] has not been easy. Between the nightmares (they're so real!), the drinking, and even moving eight times, I still have not found the answer, let alone happiness.*
> —BRAD, 40

When I think of my own feelings of depression, what I remember most is the overwhelming sense of abandonment. I felt as if others had deserted me, or that they'd forgotten that I was still grieving and were pushing me to get over it. Even worse was the feeling that my brother had also abandoned me. As I struggled with these conflicting emotions, I knew in my heart that my brother did not want to die—that he never would have left me on purpose—and I also knew that others had not been as deeply affected by my brother's death so they *did* move on. All of this made it difficult for me talk to others, to reach out to my husband and friends for help, so I usually ended up feeling resentful, alone, and, at times, very depressed.

> *Our mother died in 1990 and our father died in 1996. Although I missed them both, I could accept their passing because they had lived full lives and were ready to go (both were in their mid-eighties). My brother's death in 1997 was another thing entirely. We had bonded together more than ever during our father's dying process, and we had vowed to be closer and more involved with each other than before. I had anticipated a loving, mutually supportive relationship with him well into old age. Jim's [age 54] death left me feeling abandoned. I had come to feel that as my only sibling, he was the one person I could always count on to care about me. I wondered how I would carry on without him.*
>
> —JANET, 57

Notice that Janet's relationship with her brother grew stronger as together they passed through one of life's most difficult stages—the death of one's parents. Janet views her parents' deaths as tragic, yet part of the natural progression of life; her brother's death, however, was premature. Jim's death left Janet as the sole survivor of her immediate family, shattering her long-held belief that they would grow old together.

Because siblings are united by a common bond forged in childhood, we live with the *expectation* that we'll somehow always be together as we journey through life. Oh, we may divert from the common family path from time to time to pursue our own callings, but only our brothers and sisters know the way back to that original road where, together, we began our odyssey. In an uncertain world that is ever changing, chances are that your brother or sister has been a constant in your life, all your life. Losing a sibling, then, destroys the illusion of permanence in a more profound way than most other deaths. Indeed, we take for granted that our siblings will be there to help us cope with the death of our parents, and we assume that our siblings, who are usually close to us in age, will grow old alongside us. Naturally, we feel abandoned when this assumption is decimated by death. Of course, abandonment issues are particularly difficult when, like Janet and Julie, you've lost your *only* sibling.

> *Bill [age 26] was my only sibling, so that makes me an only sur-*
> *viving sibling or an only surviving child to my parents. My role*
> *as a sister in this world had ended. I do not mean to say that my*
> *loss or grief is greater, but it is different than those who have*
> *other siblings. I feel so much responsibility for my parents. When*
> *they die, I will lose another part of Bill.*   —JULIE, 37

Another factor that may contribute to your depression is the number of previous losses you've endured. Depending upon your age, you may have already lost one or both parents, possibly a spouse, friends, other family members, coworkers, neighbors, or pets. You may barely begin to recover from one loss before you're forced to deal with another.

> *My father died in March 1984; my mother died in May 1985;*
> *my sister died in July 1986; and then a close friend died in May*
> *1987. There was no time to process and recover from one death*
> *before another one happened. The pain was overwhelming.*
> —KATHY-ANNE, 53

Many surviving siblings report that they feel almost *stalked* by death. In a recent conversation with my colleague and friend Elaine, we observed that some families seem to have more than their share of losses, while others seem not to have any at all. We agreed there seems to be some cosmic imbalance at work in the universe that neither of us, despite our advanced degrees in theology, could begin to understand.

I lost three brothers within a twenty-seven-month period, all in accidents. Eddie [age 46] died in a grain-bin accident, Dennis [age 34] died in a train wreck, and his twin brother, Dwayne [age 36 at the time of his death], died in a chemical explosion. Dwayne's death was particularly difficult. The twins (Dennis and Dwayne) were born when I was seven, and I felt more like a mother to Dwayne. He was mischievous, and I was always defending him. He was married and had two children, ages five and eight. When my first brother, Dennis, was killed, there was a great deal of support from my large (seven children) family. He had not married, so there was no wife and children to feel sorry for. He lived five hundred miles away and did not come home very often, even for the holidays, so it just seemed like he never came home. Eddie was three years older than me and was married with three grown children. I miss him and feel especially sorry for his wife, who seems very sad and lonely. Eddie's three children still have a difficult time attending family functions, even today. There were so many feelings and frustrations accumulated that there wasn't time to deal with all of them. I woke up crying many mornings and felt quite depressed. I went to my doctor, and he prescribed something and told me to go to counseling. I never filled the prescription, but I did go to a grief recovery group sponsored by a funeral home in our area. I found it very helpful.

—JAN, 56

I don't know why some people suffer more loss, more death, and more than their share of heartache. I don't know how some people are able to go on in the face of such overwhelming tragedy, but most do. Of course, there are many times when I feel like giving in to the depression, and sometimes I do. But I try not to allow myself to remain in the pit of despair for too long; the further down you go, the harder it is to climb back to the top.

• • •

It's been four months since my brother's death, and my husband is about to turn forty. His six siblings and parents arrange a family reunion in South Carolina to celebrate his birthday. When I tell my friend Anne about our proposed trip, she sounds worried. "Are you sure you're up for this?" she asks. "Of course I am," I say without hesitation. "Why wouldn't I be?"

Anne chooses her words carefully. "I know you want Rob to celebrate his birthday with his family," she says slowly, "but I'm just concerned that it's too soon for you to be around people—especially happy siblings—laughing and having a grand old time when your heart is breaking." Initially, I feel slightly annoyed by Anne's suggestion that I'm somehow too depressed to be around normal people, but then I have a sinking feeling she's right. I panic at the thought of spending four days with energetic, carefree people when all I want to do is crawl into bed and pull the covers over my head.

Days later, I mention to my husband the possibility of staying behind and not going to Charleston with the rest of the family, but he looks so disappointed that I immediately retract my proposition. "You'll be all right," he promises. "Besides," he adds with all sincerity, "it'll be good for you. Maybe it will help you to cheer up." I smile weakly and think, "He really doesn't get it at all."

During the weeks before the trip, I become increasingly anxious and moody. I have a series of disturbing nightmares that make no sense—gruesome images of old people in hospital beds with terrible wounds, strange people crying in huddled little masses, bizarre religious dreams—and though none of the dreams address my brother's death in a direct way, I sense they're somehow connected to his passing. Naturally, I have trouble sleeping; and when I do sleep, it's not very productive. I toss and turn and wake up crying. I grow impatient with the depression and begin to view it as a character flaw. "Snap out of it!" I say to myself when I'm feeling low; but this only makes me feel worse.

The trip to Charleston comes at the lowest point in my grief journey; to this day, I can't remember most of what went on during those four long days. We arrive late in the afternoon, and everyone seems so glad to see us. This *should* make me feel better, but it doesn't. "How can they be so cheerful when my brother is dead?" I wonder miserably. Of course, I end up feeling guilty, self-absorbed, and inadequate for harboring such thoughts. After all, my husband's family barely knew my brother; most of them had only met him once or twice. Intellectually, I know I can't expect them to understand the depth of my loss—but then, I'm not thinking rationally.

So I smile and feign interest in whatever we're doing; by the end of the day, I'm physically and emotionally exhausted from keeping up the pretense of normalcy. Fortunately, no one really seems to notice, except for my sister-in-law, N. J., who's married to my husband's younger brother. She's no stranger to grief, having recently lost her mother. She offers me sympathetic smiles when my eyes betray sadness.

One evening, after dinner, my husband and his siblings gather around the piano to sing in much they same way they did as children. Their eclectic repertoire ranges from show tunes to Beatles songs, and I know from experience that the singing may go on for hours. I sit in an adjacent room with the other "outlaws" drinking beer and talking about nothing in particular. Eventually, there's a lull in the conversation; then my favorite Beatles song, "If I Fell," fills the air, and I'm struck by the near-perfect blending of sibling voices, harmonizing in that special way only siblings can. A stab of sorrow reminds me that I'll never sing with *my* brother again. The tears threaten then, so I leave the room and step outside into the warm summer night.

The air is muggy and filled with the buzz of ferocious southern insects. Standing alone on the porch in the darkness, I look up as wispy night clouds part, showing off a nearly full moon. The sky, framed by treetops and studded with blinking stars, seems vast and infinite, yet only a preamble to the universe that stretches further beyond my reckoning. All at once, I know with great certainty that my brother is now a part of that universe, but at the same time, still very much a part of me. A quiet peace fills the empty places within my soul, as I finally believe what I have taught my students for so many years: that love survives even the pain of death. I lean against the railing, close my eyes, and whisper softly, "I miss you," and my words are carried off into the night.

WHAT HELPS

Two years before my brother died, one of my old college chums, Jackie, died of cancer. Jackie's death was a terrible loss; she was a young mother with a loving husband and a promising career. I grieved terribly and felt depressed for months. One night, feeling particularly sad and low, I phoned my brother. He listened patiently as I shared my grief with him and encouraged me to talk about Jackie and what she meant to me. Before we hung up, my brother told me, "I know that when you're feeling depressed, it's hard to imagine you'll ever feel better again, but you will." At the time, I had difficulty believing him, but he was right; over time, I *did* feel better. How ironic that my brother's words would also comfort me in my struggle with depression following his own death. And now, I offer you the same hope that things will get better. In fact, even though you may feel weak, defeated, and hopeless right now, there are several things you can do to help yourself better cope with depression.

First, try to learn as much as you can about depression. Aside from your local mental health facility, there are scores of online resources and books to help you understand grief-related depression and ways to cope with the various symptoms (see "Chapter Resources" in the appendix).

Second, know your triggers. Triggers include such things as

holidays, birthdays, death anniversaries, special songs, and special places—anything that causes you to fall into a depressed state. For me, one of my worst triggers was going to church. In fact, I couldn't go to church for months after my brother died without feeling depressed for days afterward. It was the songs. The spiritual music that had in the past uplifted me now triggered terrible bouts of depression.

I tried going to a support group but stopped because it made me cry for the rest of the day. I've quit going to church because all I do is cry uncontrollably. My family still tells me, "Debbie, you've just got to get over this. There's nothing that you can do about it." But how could they understand? Lori [age 31] was the only person I could tell anything to. She was my best friend. Every time something good or something bad happened, I would pick up the phone and tell her. I can't do that anymore. I still feel very alone, like a part of me died and will never return.

—DEBBIE, 37

Holidays are very hard. And, of course, news of Kathleen's [age 29] killer still appears in the media, which really affects me. Stories of other murders are also triggers for my pain.

—MARY, 52

One way to avoid the depression precipitated by a trigger is to plan ahead. For instance, if you know your sister's birthday is going to be a difficult day for you, plan to do something life-affirming on that day, like planting a rosebush in her memory or releasing helium-filled balloons, one for each year she lived, into the air. Inform others who care about you that a trigger day is approaching and ask for their support.

On Mother's Day each year, I buy something little that I think Andy [age 22] might have given to our mother. I've told my mother that there probably aren't many things Andy misses about life on this earth, but that buying her gifts is surely one of them. I give it to her right in the bag, the way he always did. I include a short note, thanking her for always loving him and never giving up on him. I also send my mother a card on the anniversary of Andy's death and on his birthday every year. When I lived near her, I had her over for dinner, and we even had cake to celebrate. On Christmas, I take homemade cookies to Andy's grave. He loved animals, and I like the thought of deer or rabbits resting where Andy's body rests.

—LISA-MARIE, 34

The Compassionate Friends was a helpful support group for me. Our chapter has an active sibling group. Most of my old friends have stopped asking about Bill's [age 26] death and my feelings. My new compassionate friends are the only people who remember the tough days, such as birthdays, holidays, and anniversaries.

—JULIE, 37

Naturally, there are certain triggers we can't anticipate, such as the death of another loved one. Because the wounds from our previous losses are often reopened each time we experience another death, you're more likely to fall into a depression whenever you're faced with another loss, as in Sean's sad story.

Ten months after Kel [age 33] passed, my three-month-old daughter, Siobhan Kelly, died in her sleep. I was still grieving for Kel at that time. My family had just completed and turned in a panel for the AIDS Quilt, and we were still trying to comprehend losing Kel. Another brother's daughter died sixteen months later. There have been many high and low spots along the way, but I never get used to not seeing, hugging, and hearing my little brother Kelly. I miss his good humor and loving, funny ways. I've known him since I was a baby, and we had secrets, stories, and funny memories that only we could share. I pray for him every day, thanking him for all he did for me, and I give thanks for our time together. I talk to him and tell him that I love and miss him and will be glad to see him again. —SEAN, 40

There's no way to prepare for a sudden death, of course, but I think it's important to be aware that any new loss may rekindle feelings of intense grief and depression. One surviving sister told me, "I recently attended the funeral of a neighbor whom I did not know very well, but I think I cried more than his widow! It took me awhile to realize that I was actually regrieving my sister's sudden death two years before. The whole episode left me depressed for weeks."

Many surviving siblings find that simply spending time with loved ones and talking about their feelings brings the most relief. When you're depressed, often the inclination is to withdraw; if at all possible, however, I urge you to reach out to others during this time. If you've established a relationship with a grief partner, his or her counsel and listening presence will be immensely helpful. Try to make an effort to stay in touch with friends and family members, especially those who knew your sibling, since they are more likely to understand how you're feeling.

My family has always been close, so when Kel died, we leaned on each other. I think we were good at listening and understanding what each family member was going through. Family, dear friends, and even coworkers listened to me, checked on me, and helped to ease my pain. More than anyone, though, my wife, Chris, and little boy, Cael, carried me through the dark times. Chris had known Kel for as long as she knew me. She was hurting badly, too. But so many mornings, she would awake and hear me crying in another room and then come and hold me.

—SEAN, 40

In addition to recognizing your triggers and communicating your feelings to others, try to remain active. Exercise, even a short walk every day, can release positive energies (or endorphins) that help to counteract some of the sluggishness often associated with depression. I remember days when I could only manage a ten-minute walk, but I'm convinced it helped to lift my mood a little. Journaling and other creative activities can also be quite beneficial; try to keep up outside interests and hobbies as much as possible. I like to think of these outside activities as *grief breaks*, or temporary hiatuses from the pain of depression. It's a good idea to try to schedule at least one prearranged grief break each day. In addition to my daily walk, I found reading to be an easy and engaging respite from the intensity of grief and depression.

> *I accepted activities at my church and kept up the garden and flowers and yard work at home. A widow neighbor and I began to do things together and help some older neighbors. All of these activities helped my depression.* —DOROTHY, 81

But what if, despite your best efforts, the depression doesn't seem to be getting any better? The focus here has been on the so-called normal grief responses as outlined by Dr. Wolfelt, but if you suspect you're suffering from a more severe form of depression, how do you begin to search for help? The best place to start is with your family physician. Your doctor can rule out any physical problems that might be contributing to your depression (or even masquerading as depression when a physical ailment is really to blame).

> *I was already under a great deal of stress before September 11. My company was a dot-com located in downtown New York City. The company went bust, and I was the officer responsible for administering and selling off assets during our bankruptcy, so*

when the terrorist attacks happened, it was the last straw. I spent weeks fighting the lack of concentration and a whole host of grief/depression symptoms before I finally went to my doctor, who diagnosed depression and PTSD [post-traumatic stress disorder].   —KATHY B., 37

Kathy was wise to begin with her doctor, who was able to diagnose that she was suffering from post-traumatic stress disorder (PTSD). Generally speaking, post-traumatic stress disorder is a serious psychiatric disorder associated with a major trauma that is particularly horrifying or frightening. Most people think of veterans experiencing war flashbacks when they reflect on PTSD, but this condition is not limited to the survivors of the terrifying events of war. PTSD can result from a trauma related to the death of another and often occurs with depression. Following the terrorist attacks of September 11, 2001, many people, especially in the New York City area, were diagnosed with PTSD. Of course, only a physician is qualified to diagnose and treat this disorder.

If your doctor determines that you are indeed depressed, he or she will probably recommend a therapist most suited to your particular needs and may even prescribe medication. You can help your doctor by being clear about your expectations and needs regarding therapy. Make a list of requirements and questions regarding therapy and bring the list with you to your doctor's appointment. For example, you should include such things as how much you're able to pay (in some cases, insurance companies are unwilling to pay for counseling), whether you prefer a counselor of the same gender, and whether you're more interested in group therapy, individual therapy, or both. Your doctor should also be able to help you wade through the alphabet soup of credentials associated with the various types of therapists. Many grief counselors have the Association for Death Education and Counseling (ADEC) credential, which designates specific training in bereavement counseling. This is not to say, of course, that all who lack this credential are incapable of providing good grief therapy, only that the ADEC qualification serves as a good general starting point in your search for a therapist. Most people are surprised when they learn that anyone can call him- or herself a therapist or a counselor. In many states, the industry seems grossly unregulated; a competent physician can help you choose a therapist who is both licensed and experienced in the area of grief counseling.

Once you connect with a therapist or a bereavement group, you're likely to find a great deal of comfort in sharing your feelings with others who understand what it means to grieve.

I asked for and received a lot of professional counseling, during which I recognized how much the loss of my brother changed everything for me. —BETTY, 75

I attended a ten-week suicide survivors group with my mom and older sister, which brought great relief.

—VICTORIA, 26

While many surviving siblings experience an almost immediate relief in sharing their feelings, others complain they actually feel worse after a session and may even give up on the idea of therapy after only one or two sessions. Although it's difficult to be patient when you're feeling depressed, it's important to remember that in most cases, relief doesn't happen right away. Try to remind yourself that therapy is a process; healing can best be described as more of a gradual evolution rather than an instantaneous cure.

Finally, I sought counseling. It didn't bring relief right away, but it was very helpful to at least know that what I was experiencing was clinical depression and that it is a common stage in the grieving process. I chose not to be medicated, but the counseling sessions, combined with the passage of time, did help me to come out of it. Although it is difficult for me to say precisely when it started and ended, my depression lasted about five to six months. —DEAN, 30

In any discussion of therapy, the question of whether to use medication inevitably arises. There's a great deal of controversy surrounding the use of certain medications in the treatment of depression, and some surviving siblings choose to be medicated, while others do not. I strongly believe this is an issue that should be evaluated on a case-by-case basis after considerable consultation with your physician.

I was already dealing with a lot of previously repressed sadness, grief, and sense of loss about my parents' deaths and had made good progress, I thought, when my brother's death occurred. Allen's [age 31] death seemed to throw me right back into the hole I was crawling out of. I never took medication and am generally opposed to psychiatry's reliance on high-profit, quick pharmaceutical cures for what I consider to be life problems/issues. —B. G., 49

Although most surviving siblings who seek counseling find it helpful, others find the opposite to be true. For some, therapy only serves to exacerbate their grief. This may be due to a variety of factors, ranging from the individual therapist and his or her particular therapeutic approach to feeling like the odd person out in a group therapy session in which you are the only person who has lost a sibling. In cases such as these, it's probably a good idea to shop around a little more. Often, personalities simply don't mesh. For example, a perfectly fine therapist can simply rub you the wrong way, or a bereavement group might be led by a minister you don't like. There's really nothing you can do in such circumstances, other than find a different therapist or bereavement group.

Aside from the personality/therapeutic-approach issues, however, the fact remains that for some people, therapy and bereavement groups just aren't helpful. I've tried to stress the importance in honoring grieving differences, and here is a case in point.

> *I went to grief counseling, and they kept insisting that I needed to cry. I could not do it. They said that I would see no progress unless I allowed myself to cry. It took me a year and a half before I really cried. I was not medicated, and the frozen feelings of grief persisted for years. Nobody taught me how to release them. I began overeating to not feel the pain and gained forty pounds. It is still a painful topic, even twelve years later.*
>
> —KATHY-ANNE, 53

Although counseling isn't for everyone, if you're clinically depressed (and even if you're not), it can be a great source of support and healing. At the very least, it provides a forum for you to vent your feelings in a safe, nonjudgmental environment.

> *I joined a grief support group. Didn't think it helped much except it was a place that allowed me to talk about Gail [age 40]. I didn't want to keep bothering my friends and family, although they tried to be supportive.* —HARRI, 50

Although I focus primarily on the benefits of traditional therapy and bereavement groups, there are plenty of other alternative therapies from which to choose. For instance, pastoral or spiritual counseling, which combines elements of traditional psychology and spirituality, has become quite popular. Many priests, rabbis, and ministers have additional training in grief-related issues, and many outside the clergy are qualified to offer pastoral/spiritual counseling as well. If you're interested in a counselor affiliated with a particular religious denomination, ask your clergyperson for a referral (there are also nondenominational pastoral/spiritual counselors).

Other alternative therapies, ranging from holistic counseling to Chinese medicine, are also available. Most nontraditional therapies have a national organization dedicated to maintaining professional standards, so if you're having difficulty in locating a practitioner in your area, this may be the best place to begin (see "Chapter Resources" in the appendix). The types and styles of alternative approaches to treating depression could be the subject of an entire book, so my mention of it here is simply to make you aware that there are other treatment options available. Finally, don't feel as if you're limited to just one particular form of therapy. Many surviving siblings try a variety of coping techniques before finding one that brings relief.

My mother and I took Valium for six to eight weeks. I wish I could have taken a year off. My whole life, my everyday life, was blown apart. I did seek counseling. I started yoga and acupuncture, and I wrote in a journal. I read a lot of grief books, and I kept a gratitude journal to remind me that every day some things did go right. I was hanging on by a thread. I joined a gospel singing class. All of these things helped, but my family and friends helped the most. I'm training for the San Francisco Marathon. I've never done anything like this before. The program and the exercise routine have been incredible. Definitely helps with depression. —KATHLEEN, 39

It's important to understand that depending upon the severity and type of depression, no one treatment option is necessarily better than another. In my own journey through depression, I investigated several options, ranging from individual and group therapy to acupuncture treatments, but I eventually abandoned the idea of grief therapy altogether and decided to gut it out on my own. In retrospect, I'm not so sure this was the best thing for me, but at the time, I was just too tired and too confused to continue the search. What I wanted and needed most was to talk to someone—anyone—who might understand what it meant to lose a sibling. This desire to connect with other surviving siblings would later become the impetus behind both this book and the creation of the Adult Sibling Grief website (www.adultsibling grief.com), but there were many dark and desperate days before either of those came to fruition.

Remember, too, that grief is not a linear process; it's fairly common to have a delayed experience of depression that occurs months or even years after your loss. And, of course, you may also experience a recurrence of depression from time to time.

Although I can't say for certain when the depression began, I can recall when I was able to gain the upper hand in fighting it. Standing in the darkness on the porch in South Carolina and feeling a connection to my brother changed the way I had been viewing my grief. After that night, I knew that I could still have a relationship with my brother, despite the fact that he was no longer physically a part of this world. More important, I learned I did not have to let go of him to heal. In fact, the opposite was true: I needed to learn how to embrace both my loss and my brother in a new way.

8

DREAMS

One Last Visit

Dreams which are not interpreted are like letters that have not been opened.

—ERICH FROMM

I SIT AT my desk grading papers as the last of the afternoon sun casts distorted images of chairs and desks across the wall. Soon, I'm surrounded by shadows—Druids in hooded ceremonial robes—I feel tense, anxious, and filled with dread. I close my eyes and silently pray for a delay; a few more hours of sunlight, that's all I want. But the heavens ignore my plea as clouds gather darkly, signaling the approach of evening.

I collect my work, shove it into my briefcase, and pretend not to notice the streetlights blinking on as I hurry to my car. Driving home, I ignore the lights warming the living rooms of houses as I drive past. I turn on the radio and sing along as if the words and melodies mean something special to me. Finally, at home, I draw the blinds and turn on every light in the house. (No one says anything about this, though my daughter appears at the dinner table wearing sunglasses.) Stirring pots in my kitchen as Oprah gives advice, I eventually accept defeat. Nighttime has come, despite my efforts to forestall its arrival. As I serve my family dinner, I try to console myself by believing that this night will somehow be different.

. . .

Many years ago, I watched a television program about medical residents in training and the toll sleep deprivation takes on both their physical and emotional health. I learned that residents often go days, sometimes weeks, without adequate sleep and that the lack of sleep can often impair their judgment. "How can anyone function after a week of not sleeping?" I asked my husband, who was watching the program next to me. We talked about sleep deprivation, and I concluded that it would be impossible for any-one, even those hardy young doctors in training, to function nor-mally without regular sleep. The program had to be presenting an exaggerated picture of the life of medical residents. Now, years later, I know just how accurate that picture may have been—how it *is* possible to function through sleep deprivation. I know this because for the five months following my brother's death, I've barely slept at all.

Lack of sleep affects me on a variety of levels. An active family and demanding career leave me tired at the end of the day; I need my sleep to be both a successful parent and teacher. Within a month after my brother's death, I'm falling behind at work, and I have trouble concentrating. Little things that in the past never bothered me are suddenly irksome; unprepared students and endless, nonproductive meetings top the list. At home, my children remind me to write down important dates, like play practice and basketball games; they quickly adjust to the memory lapses and crankiness that are the by-products of my sleep deprivation.

I have problems both falling asleep and staying asleep. Most nights I struggle to sleep at all. If I do sleep, it's never for more than a couple of hours. Eventually, I resign myself to the fact that sleeplessness, at least for me, is somehow part of the pack-age of grieving.

I spend many long nights huddled on the overstuffed chair by the living room window, an interloper in the quiet stillness of my sleeping house. I envy my husband and children as they dream peacefully in the comfort of their beds upstairs. My only com-pany on these nights is our old, gray-faced golden retriever, Katie, whose tail thumps a greeting as I pad down the stairs past her bed in the kitchen. Sometimes I sit with her for a while and talk quietly to her. Her soft, expressive brown eyes seem to sense my sadness, and she looks at me as if to say, "I know you're tired and sad, but I'm here with you."

I gaze out the window into the night at the houses and the cars on my street, imagining my friends and neighbors slumbering without worry or care, their lives awash in perfect bliss. What bothers me most about not sleeping, however, is not the persistent fatigue or the loneliness of the night. What bothers me most is my inability to dream.

I miss my brother so much; I long to see him, to hug him, just one more time. But with each passing day, I feel him moving further and further away from my memory. I tell myself that perhaps he'll visit me in a dream, and I'm immediately buoyed by this thought. Soon I convince myself that in order to feel whole again, I *must* have a dream about my brother, one final visit.

The desire to meet my brother in a dream becomes a sort of project for me. I read books on insomnia, take various herbal sleeping aids, and drink teas with sleepy-sounding names. I try staying up late so that sheer exhaustion might allow me to sleep. I take warm baths with a mug of hot milk, and then I try combining the two, taking warm *milk* baths. I spend a great deal of time learning to meditate, hoping to clear my mind of the clutter that keeps me awake and pacing the floor late into the night. I read books about dreams and memorize techniques for recalling them. I sleep with headphones on, lulled by New Age music designed to lure dreams from the depths of the unconscious. And I pray each night for a dream: "Even a short dream, God," I plead. "I'll take anything." But sadly, no dream comes to me.

Other family members and friends of my brother have already had dreams about him, and they excitedly share the details of these moments with me. Try as I might to feel happy for them, I'm unable to feel anything but envy. My sister Tracy has a wonderfully uplifting dream about our brother, and she can't wait to share it with me. She calls me early one morning and says, "I had a beautiful dream about VJay last night."

"What?" I rage inside my head, suddenly a thirteen-year-old all over again. "How can *you* have a dream about him before me?

I'm older!" I feel suddenly ashamed, and then, trying to sound encouraging, I ask her to tell me about the dream. "In the dream, I was in a room with other people, but the only person whose presence I felt was VJay. I was on one side of the room, and he was on the other. We caught each other's eye from across the room, and he looked at me with so much radiance that I wanted to cry. He looked so healthy, and I was so happy to see him again!" she says, her voice filled with emotion. As I listen to her describe her dream, an ugly pang of disappointment wells in my chest. On the one hand, I'm happy for my sister, who, just like me, is in mourning. But on the other hand, it seems somehow unfair that she should get a dream, while I have nothing but white-noise sleep, and very little of that.

After we hang up, I sit for a long time staring blankly at the floor. I wonder: Why haven't I had a dream? Does this mean that my brother loves me less than my sister? Am I afraid to have a dream about him? Is there something wrong with me? What kind of person am I, anyway, to be jealous of my own sister, who's been given the gift of dreaming about her dead brother? Is this what I've become? I feel depressed and guilty for the rest of the day.

I finally conclude that I'm not dreaming about my brother because I never sleep long enough to dream about anything. This makes me feel better, at least for a while. But then months pass, and still no dream. I reach the point where I'm actually angry when someone else has a dream about my brother. One afternoon, during a walk with my friend Nancy R., I talk excitedly about my efforts to entice a dream about my brother. I tell her about the New Age music and the meditation, about the teas and the herbal sleeping pills. "If I could just get a good night's sleep, I know I'll have a dream about my brother." Nancy stops walking and looks at me. "You need to let this dream thing go," she says soberly. "You're really getting obsessive about it." Of course, I think she's overreacting—I'm hardly obsessive about wanting a dream, I tell myself—but after a few more sleepless nights, I decide she's right. And so I make an important decision: I decide to stop trying to have a dream altogether. "Maybe I'm just not meant to have a last visit," I tell myself. "Maybe it's just not in the cards." Perhaps it's no accident that as soon as I decide to give up trying to force a dream about my brother, I actually have one.

The night begins like so many others I've experienced lately. I go to bed early, exhausted, only to wake two hours later. I read for several hours, eventually returning to my bed as the first fingers of dawn trace pink across the sky. I fall almost instantly into a deep sleep and, at last, have a dream about my brother. In the dream, my brother and I are leaning against the hood of his beloved old black Mercedes. We talk and laugh and share a bag of Swedish Fish candy. The sun is warm, and I can see his face clearly. I can't recall what we talk about in the dream, but it must be awfully funny, because we're both collapsing in laughter.

I'm still smiling when I awake from the dream, and for one brief instant, I forget that he's gone. I feel his lingering presence for most of the morning. I don't mean *presence* in an eerie or spooky sense, but the sense of energy felt between two people sitting in the same room. One person may be off in the corner reading while the other works on a crossword puzzle at the opposite side of the room, but each *feels* the presence of the other.

The other striking thing about this dream is the amount of detail I'm able to recall. The candy, Swedish Fish, one of my favorites as a child, is in a tiny white paper bag, the kind you get in expensive candy shops. I can see my brother's face so vividly—I remember his eyelashes and the squint of his eyes in the sun. He looks alive, healthy, and young. And his laughter—how wonderful it is to hear the sound of his laughter again!

The car, virtually erased from my waking memory, now appears in the dream, clean and polished, just as my brother always kept it. It all seems so *real*.

The power of this dream is not in the details, however, but rather in the sustaining presence that follows it. For days, I feel hopeful and happy. I have since learned that other surviving siblings, like Ronna, experience the same lingering effects that I felt.

> *I had one dream that I remember about Dana [age 21]. She died in my dream, but I wouldn't believe it. In the dream, I remember holding her in my arms, trying to get her to wake up, but she wouldn't. I was rocking her. What stands out the most to me is that when I woke up, I remember what it felt like to have touched her. I could recall her entire bone structure: her thin but wide shoulders, her long arms and legs. I wanted to remember everything about her. I wished I had given her a hug the last time I saw her, just to remember.* —RONNA, 34

Like Ronna, many surviving siblings describe the *presence* associated with the grief dream in terms of a lingering *physical* sensation that survives the dream. Indeed, many siblings feel that they've actually touched their deceased brother or sister in the dream and then, upon waking, feel the lasting sensation of that touch, much like the feeling you might have after shaking hands with someone or being gripped in a bear hug. I want to stress the fact that this lingering physical sensation is in no way unsettling; quite the contrary. It is a special kind of dream that energizes and sustains us in our grief.

> *I have had two amazing dreams about my brother since his death seven years ago that have changed me forever. Bob [age 33] and I were sitting underneath a big tree talking about how to comfort my parents during this difficult time. I could feel his hand holding mine as he comforted me. He assured me that things would be fine and that he was watching out for his children. Several months ago, I had a second dream. I kept rubbing my brother's hand and cried while begging him to visit my mom in a dream.*

He just smiled at me and said, "I have things to do." I have never in my life had dreams where I could feel the person there even after I woke up. I really feel that these were much more than dreams. —TAMI, 26

At times, the longing to see my brother, to hear his voice, and to just be with him is overwhelming. That wonderful initial dream, however, helped me to understand that he's still connected to me, and I will forever consider it a beautiful gift. Whether the dream was from my brother or God, or simply a product of my unconscious, really doesn't matter much to me. Whatever its origin, the dream gave me the courage to face another day without him. And since that first dream about my brother, there have been others. They seem to come at random, without marking any particular anniversaries, but much like Sean's dream, they seem to be gentle reminders that he's still a part of my life.

I have occasional dreams about Kel [age 33], mostly everyday scenarios or dreams about when we were kids. The most powerful dream I had was in the year after his death. I dreamed that I was in a post office lobby, writing at a stand-up desk. I felt a man behind me, and I knew it was one of my brothers. I turned around and saw Kel. He said, "You know that I loved you." I said, "Yes." I woke up crying, but so reassured that Kel was well and still near. —SEAN, 40

· · ·

During the latter half of that first year without my brother, I had an interesting dream that took place in a parking garage, of all places. In the dream, I see a man at a distance who looks like my brother. He wears a black trench coat and seems to be in a hurry. I run toward him and call his name, but he keeps walking and seems not to hear. The closer I get to him, the more I realize that it *is* my brother. I feel a flood of excitement and relief as I run faster to catch up to him. Finally, I come up beside him and grab his arm. "VJay!" I cry, "I thought you were dead!" He turns to face me, smiling in such a way that I have the distinct feeling he has been playing some sort of joke on me in making me chase after him. "Didn't you know it was me? Didn't you hear me calling your name?" I ask him. He chuckles and says, "Try not to worry so much. I'm fine. I'm really fine."

As I speak with more and more surviving siblings, I realize that there are many common features associated with our grief dreams. I am particularly struck by Dean's dream of Stefani and how much of it mirrors my own dreams about VJay.

I was surprised that I didn't have any dreams about Stefani [age 25] during the first couple of months following her death. Then I had seemingly insignificant dreams in which Stefani was alive, and it was as if she had never died. After a few months, I had a dream in which Stefani walked into the house and was alive. I ran to her and hugged her and told her that we thought she was dead. She said, "I know," and it was clear that she realized how serious the situation was. She was about to explain how it was that she hadn't really died and why she hadn't come to us sooner. I hugged her again, tightly. Then the dream ended. In the next dream I had about Stefani, she wasn't alive, but I was talking to her about her death. She said that she didn't want my family and me to be too sad, and I said something like, "But someone killed you." She said, "I know, but there's nothing that can be done about that." She said it in a way that showed that she was upset about it but unable to change it. She realized how terrible it was that she died, but she was concerned about us and the difficulties we were having with her death. When I awoke, I felt sad but strangely comforted, because for an instant I had been with Stefani again, communicating with her. Although my mother occasionally has nightmares about Stefani's death, I never have.

—DEAN, 30

Not all grief dreams are comforting, however. Although the vast majority of the dreams associated with the death of a brother or a sister are uplifting, consoling, even inspiring, many surviving siblings suffer from nightmares and disturbing dreams. In particular, traumatic deaths, such as murders or accidents, can trigger terrifying dreams as our subconscious replays our own version of our sibling's last moments.

> *I've had mostly nightmares, horrible dreams of Tommy [age 36], scared and dying. In my dreams, he is trying to get out of the burning building. I used to work in the World Trade Center myself, so my knowledge of the layout of the buildings has made my dreams particularly painful in detail. I sometimes dream of Tommy, choking on that oily smoke, running to the stairwells only to find them aflame; he runs to the window, frantically trying to breathe in cleaner air. Then he tries to evacuate to the roof, because if you can't evacuate down, you're supposed to evacuate up. I can see him, worried about his wife and babies, afraid he'll never see them again, never hold them again. He's trying to get home to them, but the world ends and the building collapses. I usually wake up when I feel that free-falling sensation—that sickening plunge down, surrounded by screaming tons of metal, concrete, and fellow victims.* —KATHY B., 37

But nightmares are not limited to recollections of violent deaths; watching your brother or sister suffer prior to death can induce these types of dreams, too. I still have what I call *hospital dreams* every now and then that serve as painful reminders of those last, terrible days of my brother's life. The noises and smells of the hospital, the machines, the doctors and nurses bustling about—all of this threatens to come rushing back during sleep. Occasionally, if I've been in a hospital or even find myself watching a television show set in a hospital, I'll have a hospital dream; but that type of dream is rare, and I have come to accept it as part of the process of grief.

> *Before Judith's [age 31] death from breast cancer, I remember a dream where she was inside a dark cave, pinned to the wall by a stalactite piercing her through the chest, dying. Everything was in red or black or white. She told me to get out, but I didn't want to leave her there. I had to, but it was very painful.*
>
> —ELISE, 36

I've always had a special interest in dreams and their meaning, an interest that began in childhood. In fact, my family places great value on dream interpretation and the connections of our dreams to life. Not that any of us has any formal training in this area, but both my mother and grandmother have always deciphered the meaning of dreams with great authority. For example, according to my mother, if you lose a tooth in your dream, it means that either you want to have a baby or that you are going to have a baby (when my mother interpreted this particular dream for me when I was ten, I was mortified for weeks, having only just learned the process involved in conceiving a baby); if you dream that you're flying, it means good luck, but if you fall down in your dream, then bad luck is on the horizon.

This fascination with dreams continued for me well into college. When I studied Carl Jung's work on dreams, I realized that my mother and grandmother were not entirely off base in many of their dream interpretations. Jung believed that dreams were symbolic and brought healing to the psyche. He also believed that a dream was "a little hidden door [to] the innermost . . . secret recesses of the soul."

Very little clinical research has been done in the area of grief-related dreams, but since so many surviving brothers and sisters have found some measure of comfort in their dreams, it seems to me that no discussion of grief would be complete without at least some mention of this subject. Indeed, some of the most powerful, healing words uttered to surviving siblings come not from ministers, therapists, friends, or family, but from the deceased sibling him- or herself, in the form of a dream. J. Elizabeth's dream about Nancy is particularly compelling.

> *I've had a lot of dreams of Nancy [age 40], many of which involve her being there but not being able to speak to me. My other sister believes that spirits come to us in dreams, and that Nancy is really there, communicating in her own way. But the most interesting dream I had was this one: I was standing at the foot of a mountain, cradling a baby in my arms (my own child). There were other people around, telling me that I had to give up the baby, climb the mountain with a few other people, and then jump off. I was very upset, not wanting to let go of the infant, not wanting to jump off of the mountain and possibly die, leaving the baby motherless. But the others kept hounding me, and one woman held out her arms expectantly for the child. It was then that I looked down at the baby's face; it was my sister Nancy, looking back up at me. My interpretation of the dream is that Nancy was telling me that it was okay to let go of my need for her, to go ahead and live my life, as scary as it might seem (like jumping off a cliff). I still wanted to cling to her, to take care of her even though she was gone, but somehow I had to join the living and start climbing the road of life on my own.*
>
> —J. ELIZABETH, 31

I'd like to think that there's a spiritual connection wrapped up in the dreams I have of my brother, and while there's certainly a spiritual element present in them, there's something transformative about the dreams, too. I'm slowly learning that my brother will forever remain a part of my life, despite the pain of separation I so often feel. My dreams help to solidify my growing contention that death does not sever the life bond we've shared with our siblings, and so I've come to view them as blessings.

I have asked for and waited for dreams of Jim [age 54], but there has been only one in the eight months since his death. I dreamed I saw him in a public place in rather ordinary circumstances. He seemed to be waiting for something to happen or waiting to go somewhere. He was young, healthy, and very much alive, but rather impatient. I stood before him and said, "I would like to stay here and just look at you for a few minutes." In the dream, I knew he was dead, and I wanted to prolong this very vivid experience of being in his presence once again. It was an overwhelmingly beautiful experience, and I awoke feeling as if I had just received a great gift. —JANET, 57

As time passes, my dreams about my brother change. When I first began to dream about him, he was featured prominently in my dreams; sometimes offering advice or words of comfort. He was, in a way, the *star* of my dreams. Over time, however, he appears less and less in my dreams; and when he is there, he is almost always in the background, a face in the crowd. He usually does not speak, but I know that he's there. In a very real way, his presence in my dreams defines my journey of grief: intense and needy at first, and then, over time, quiet acceptance and, finally, peace.

I dreamed that I was standing at my brother's grave, crying. Jimmy came up beside me and put his arm around me and said, "I'm okay." Then he said, "Look out there." He pointed to a beautiful view of mountains and a clear blue sky. "That's where I'll always be." The dream was so real to me that I started to accept his death after that. I guess that's what I needed. One last visit. —SHERRY, 47

WHAT HELPS

Most surviving siblings are comforted by dreams of their deceased brother or sister. Dreams help to maintain a connection to our sibling at a time when letting go seems nearly impossible. In grief, we generally move forward in small, incremental steps. There are times when we may feel as if we are not moving forward at all, but we usually are. As we gradually navigate our way through bereavement, our dreams can actually ease the intensity of grief, gently helping us to accept and integrate our loss into our lives.

Under normal circumstances, understanding our dreams is rarely of paramount importance; most of us, myself included, rarely even remember their dreams. But the dreams that follow the death of a sibling are different; even people who have never thought much about dream interpretation are suddenly interested in understanding the meaning attached to their dreams. These grief dreams become enormously important as we search them for hidden messages.

Shortly after I returned from my older sister's [Paula, age 59] funeral, I saw her in a dream. She and my mom (who died eleven years ago) were walking along a country road, arm in arm. They were smiling and chatting, and I just walked up and took Mom's arm and we went on, laughing. The trees were swaying and the sun was shining on us; I could feel it. It was the most peaceful dream I can ever recall. Mom looked like she had in the late 1950s, wearing the sleeveless, brown-and-white printed sundress she often wore on warm days. I rarely have such clear dreams. I felt comforted, but disturbed at the same time. Since I had taken her arm in the dream, did this mean that I was next?

—MARTHA, 46

Many grieving siblings report that although they were never able to recall their dreams prior to their brother's or sister's death, they are now able to remember many of their dreams in great detail. One explanation for this may be that sleep patterns tend to change during bereavement. That is, grieving people generally have frequent periods of wakefulness that actually allow them to remember their dreams. People who claim they never dream simply fail to wake up enough following the dream to remember them. Some dreams last only about ten minutes, while others can last upwards of an hour. Most of us experience a new dream period every ninety minutes or so. Even though you may be having difficulty sleeping, the good news is that if you happen to dream about your brother or sister, you're likely to remember it. This is vitally important because the first step involved in deciphering your dreams is to remember them.

If you're interested in trying to recall and analyze your dreams, the best way to begin is to keep a dream journal. This can be part of your grief journal, or you can devote a different journal to this purpose. (I found that keeping my grief journal next to my bed and using it, rather than a separate journal, simply made more sense.) Place a small light or flashlight and a pen within easy reach. If you're not thrilled about the prospect of turning on the lights and writing in a journal at 2:00 A.M., you might opt for a mini cassette recorder instead. Most are affordable and simple to use.

Whatever method you use, try to set down every detail you're able to recall and be certain to record all dreams, even those dreams not specifically about your brother or sister. Don't wait until the morning to attempt to record your dreams, because by then you will have forgotten many of the important details. I found it easier to write down key phrases or words along with the general "plot" of the dream, rather than writing long, detailed scenarios.

Once you've learned to accurately record your dreams, you can then try your hand at interpreting them. For this, I'd recommend a good dream dictionary, as well as a solid book on dream interpretation (see "Chapter Resources" in the appendix). Contrary to popular belief, you don't need to be an expert in the area of dream interpretation in order to have a go at deciphering your own dreams. Of course, disturbing dreams, particularly if they tend to recur, should be discussed with your doctor or therapist.

Although it's exciting to think that our brother or sister may be communicating with us through our dreams, dream interpretation can also serve a more utilitarian purpose: Learning to understand the meaning of your dreams will help put you in touch with the aspects of grief that may be preventing you from moving forward. For example, nearly a year after my brother's death, I had a dream that I was giving a party and my brother was there. People kept talking to me, preventing me from crossing the room to spend time with him. I could see my brother standing alone on the edge of the crowd, but I couldn't get to him. I started to cry out of the sheer frustration involved in trying to push through the throng of partyers. I also felt guilty about his being alone with no one to talk to, although he did not seem perturbed by this. Finally, I yelled, "I'm trying to get to you!" across the room, and he returned a little "It's okay" wave. And then I woke up.

Later, when I thought about this dream, I realized it was probably connected to the guilt I still carried for leaving my brother before he died. Although the dream was a painful one, it helped me to realize that guilt was more of a factor in my grief than I thought, although it would be years before I actually let it go.

Most of us would like to believe that our siblings appear in our dreams by choice, to spend time with us or to deliver a special message. There is absolutely no reason to discount this possibility. No one, including the so-called experts, knows for certain just what, if anything, happens to us after we die. The possibilities and theories of life after death are endless: some are faith based, complete with elaborate paradigms and complex theologies; others negate the possibility of life after death from a purely scientific perspective. But dreams, like beliefs, depend less on the opinions of experts and more on the meaning we attach to them. If we believe that our sibling has come to us in a dream, then it is true; it is *our* truth, and scientific or religious "proofs" are largely unimportant.

About a week after my sister, Lois [age 30], died, I had a dream that we were sitting in her house talking, and I told her how sorry I was that she wouldn't be here anymore. She said that she was very, very tired and needed to rest. I said that I was worried about her husband and her two little girls, and she told me not to worry—they would be fine. The next day, I told her husband about the dream, and he said that since she had a miscarriage about a year before, she had been tired a lot of the time. The dream brought us both a little comfort.

—RAE ELLEN, 53

On Christmas Eve, Tom's [age 36] wife and daughters came over and I videotaped little Sara dancing and singing her favorite nursery rhyme. Later, I had a dream that I watched the tape, and in it I saw Tommy sitting on the couch, smiling at Sara and nodding along as she whirled around laughing and singing "Here we go 'round the mulberry bush." When I woke up, it took me a few minutes to realize I hadn't yet reviewed that tape in real life—that it was all a dream. I felt so peaceful and yet so sad. I know Tommy is watching over his two baby girls, and to me this dream was merely his way of proving it.

—KATHY B., 37

Finally, discuss your dreams (or lack of dreams) with your grief partner or trusted friend. Sharing your dreams with someone else and discussing the possible messages and meanings of your dreams can be immensely therapeutic, and it will enable your grief partner to know and understand you better. In the same way, sharing your anxiety and disappointment over *not* having dreams of your sibling is also helpful. For surviving siblings who have not yet had a dream about their brother or sister, my advice is to try to be patient. I know how important it is to you and how immensely comforting it can be to have a dream about your sibling. I also know the disappointment associated with not having such dreams. But a dream *will* come, probably when you least expect it.

I have had some comfort dreams about my brother, but not until a year after he died. In one dream, I dreamed that I woke up, wrapped in a quilt, warm and comfortable, aboard a big sailboat, the morning sun waking me. I got up and walked up the stairs to the deck, and with each step, a puff of stars sparkled around my feet. I got up on the deck and saw my brother [Sean, 43] cooking breakfast. I said, "Are we dead?" and he said, "Yes. We're going on a long journey together just to catch up on things."
                                                        —ROSEMARY, 51

9

FAITH, RELIGION, AND SPIRITUALITY

Where's God in All of This?

Out of my distress I called to the Lord, and he answered me.

—JONAH 2:3

M Y LOSS of faith happened so quietly and, yes, so naturally that it took me a while to realize it was gone. But like a rowboat not securely fastened to the dock, one moment it was there, and the next it had simply slipped away. I suspect the drifting away took place over time, beginning perhaps during those first terrible hours of shock and horror following the news of my brother's death. Yet it wasn't until several weeks later, alone in my room, attempting to pray, that I knew for certain.

On that particular night, when I called out to God in the familiar words that have drawn God to me ever since I was a child, the connection failed. I lifted my head and rubbed my temples. *What's wrong?* Taking a deep breath, I tried again. But my words seemed suddenly artificial and insincere. All at once, I saw myself, as if from a distance, head bent in an empty prayer that God does not hear. The usual warm feeling of divine embrace was instead replaced by a void so vast and silent that it took me a moment to understand what had happened. And then it hit me: I've lost my faith. I'm a babbling impostor, masquerading as a believer. And God doesn't have time for pitiable phonies like me. He's pulled up his tent stakes and moved on to the greener pastures of those who truly believe.

I considered this for a few minutes in an abstract, almost intellectual way. "So *this* is what it feels like to lose your faith," I mused curiously. My loss of faith was actually less shocking than my reaction to it; I really didn't care. The lifelong love affair with God, the years of academic theological study, those priceless "ah-ha moments" in the classroom when students finally understood the connection between faith and religion—all gone. And I didn't care.

Even God's abandonment seemed small in comparison to my brother's death.

I rose from my place on the bed, switched off the lights, and looked out the window into the night. On the corner, a streetlight glowed reassuringly, spilling soft, milky light onto the street below. My eyes were drawn to the bulb that peeked from beneath the metal hood. I was mesmerized by the bulb, which was surrounded by an aura of yellow and blue, just like a distant star.

Suddenly, the light flickered brighter, then dimmed, and then burned out altogether.

• • •

C. S. Lewis (*A Grief Observed*) wrote that grief feels very much like being afraid. I'd have to agree, but let's take his observation one step further: when we're grieving, we *are* afraid. In grief, no matter what you're doing, no matter how thoroughly engaged you may be in work, study, or conversation, there remains an uneasy feeling of *expectancy*—an on-edge sensation—as if something terrible is about to happen. And then you're constantly reminded—oh yes—something terrible *has* happened and there's nothing you can do to change it. From the moment you wake up in the morning until you close your eyes at night, fear—and all its attendant physical and emotional symptoms—intensifies the pain of grief. Soon you think you're losing your mind, but you're too afraid to tell anyone, so you avoid friends and family. Surely you can't go on feeling this way; the anxiety and misery alone will kill you. And this is something new to be feared.

Of course, there's nothing wrong with being afraid when there's something to be feared, but the biggest problem with fear is that it shatters faith.

A wise teacher once told me that the opposite of faith is

fear—and I've seen this truth played out in life. I've seen people afraid of growth and change; people afraid to take risks; people afraid of the challenges necessary to pursue their dreams; people afraid to love because they may end up getting hurt. I've watched others settle for a life of mediocrity simply because they're too afraid of failure. At one time, I couldn't understand people who are paralyzed by fear, who live life on the sidelines, too afraid to set foot on the playing field—but I understand them now. After my brother's death, I spent a long time feeling afraid. I was afraid that I wouldn't survive the sorrow; afraid that something even worse was in the offing; afraid to trust the world or God again because I had been so wrong to trust either in the first place; and afraid to admit that I was afraid.

The opposite of faith is fear.

According to the biblical interpretation, faith literally means *trust*. For example, when the biblical writers speak of an individual's *faith* in God they're really telling us about a person's *trust* in God. Before my brother's death, I would have said that I, too, trusted in God completely. But after my brother died, I found that I really didn't trust God at all.

Faith, or trust, differs from beliefs, religion, and spirituality. A belief develops when we formulate a rational understanding of a particular truth. For example, those who explain the death of your sibling in terms of "God's will" or attempt to explain your suffering as part of "God's test" are expressing their *beliefs* about who God is and isn't. You can learn a lot about people by asking about their beliefs—especially their beliefs about God. Generally speaking, the person who describes God as unforgiving, punitive, and punishing—or as loving, forgiving, and accepting—is actually describing him- or herself.

When we speak of *religion*, we're usually referring to an organized body of worshipers who share similar beliefs. Religions give rise to those beliefs through the use of sacred literature and rituals and should ideally serve to enhance and sustain the faith of believers. *Spirituality*, on the other hand, refers to the unique expression of one's faith, beliefs, and/or religion. I mention these distinctions only because although most theologians recognize differences between faith, beliefs, religion, and spirituality, most of us tend to use these terms interchangeably—and those surviving siblings who have contributed to this chapter are no exception. For our purposes, faith, belief, and spirituality will mean generally the same thing. I'll try to distinguish these from religion and religious expression, however.

My personal struggle with faith had to do with God's justice. I felt God had been terribly unfair in allowing my brother to die and for inflicting so much suffering and grief on me and my family. "How could God allow this to happen?" I lamented. I thought God and I had a special relationship; after all, I was a religion teacher, something I felt *called* to do. I had recently completed my master's degree in biblical studies, and I was a devoted wife and mother, living a more religiously observant life than most people I knew. I simply couldn't understand the apparent injustice of my brother's death. "Is this how God repays me for devoting my life to him?" I wondered bitterly. I didn't miss the irony, of course. Here was I, so smugly secure in my *preferred customer status* with God, suddenly faced with the most profound loss of my life, and God was nowhere to be found.

My brother's death caused me to question everything I've ever believed about God, faith, religion, and the meaning of life and death. Like Jonah, I descended into the belly of the beast and languished there for a while—lost, afraid, and uncertain of the person I'd be once I reemerged. At the time, I felt my questioning represented a weakness of character or, at the very least, a weakness of faith. I would later learn that questioning one's faith—even among those who profess a deep, abiding faith—is a nearly universal grief response.

Indeed, grieving people throughout the ages have tried to understand their suffering in the context of an all-loving God.

How could a God who loves us permit such suffering to enter our lives? Mystics, teachers, ministers, priests, rabbis, and much of our religious literature have tried to convince us that our suffering is merely part of God's grand design—that God's ways are mysterious, and we're simply too ignorant and unworthy to be privy to these cosmic plans. Many reasons for undeserved suffering have been put forth, such as the notion of suffering as a divine method of instruction—to teach us or others some valuable lesson—or the idea that our suffering is our just desserts, a punishment for some undefined human failing. But the bottom line is that none of these supposed reasons can be reconciled with the concept of an all-loving God. A God who loves us would not—could not—intentionally cause our suffering, for whatever divine reason.

> *I did not believe that God played a part in causing Bill [age 26] to have a defect in his brain that would someday kill him. I felt that maybe God knew that Bill was going to die, but that he simply couldn't do anything about it.* —JULIE, 37

> *God is a God of love, and he had nothing to do with Dana's [age 21] death. It wasn't "her time" and God did not "want another angel." I believe that her death was an accident and God had nothing to do with it.* —RONNA, 34

Intellectually, I knew all of this—I'd *studied* all of this. Intellectually, I also knew that God did not *cause* or *will* my brother to die. Like Julie and Ronna, I've never believed in a God who sits in heaven with a Book of Woes, arbitrarily doling out illnesses, accidents, and assorted other painful experiences to us Little People below. My studies reinforced what I intuitively knew all along and what I'd been taught as a child: Life's tragedies are not God's doing, but are simply part of being human in a less-than-perfect world. Yet in the face of profound grief, when these convictions should have sustained me, I felt like that lost rowboat, cast adrift and unable to find my way home. But why? Why did the promises of faith and religion fail me when I needed them most?

The answer can be best summarized in one word: fear. Fear challenged my faith and, quite literally, brought me to my knees. And fear is the fuel of anger. I felt confused, hurt, victimized by God, and very, very angry. I stumbled through those awful days and weeks of disbelief feeling broken and betrayed, but it took me a long time to recognize my anger. It was too difficult for me to admit that I was angry with God—and this became the Great Secret. Most of my friends, family, and colleagues wrongly assumed that because of my background in religion, I must possess a special wellspring of faith that would enable me to weather the storm of grief better than others. I'd fostered this false assumption myself, both through my external piety and in the pastoral role I often assumed with others. Images of myself in the past offering comfort and explanations to bereaved friends, family, and students suddenly flashed before me and made me wince. I wished I could go back and tell all those grieving people who turned to me with difficult questions I felt compelled to so smartly answer that I'm sorry. I didn't know anything.

• • •

I've always lived by the maxim "When the student is ready, the teacher will come." Of course, in the midst of my grief and crisis of faith, it was often difficult to recognize the many teachers who came to my rescue. But one such teacher, my friend and colleague Louise, herself a teacher of religion, helped me to examine my crisis of faith from a different perspective. She took me aside one afternoon, just before the end of the school day, and asked, "So, how are you feeling?" I shrugged and gave my stock reply: "I'm fine." She smiled and took hold of my arm to stop me from walking away. "No," she said, looking me in the eye, "how are you *really* feeling?"

I thought about changing the subject, but then, for some reason, I decided to tell her the truth. "To be perfectly honest," I said, "I'm furious. And I'm beginning to think that everything I've studied, taught, and believed about God is a lie."

Louise didn't appear surprised by this revelation at all. Instead, she said simply, "Well, it's normal to doubt those things when you're grieving. And don't worry too much about being angry at God; God can handle it."

Louise's offhand observation had a major impact on me, and I turned it over in my mind for several weeks. Could it be that my so-called loss of faith was more a symptom of grief than an actual change of heart? I now know that grief brings with it a flood of feelings and emotions, many of which we've never experienced before; some of these feelings are transient, while others reflect real changes that occur as a result of our grief journey. Sometimes, particularly in early grief, it's difficult to tell the difference. Although it would take me many more months to discern whether my crisis of faith was merely a temporary aspect of my overall grief experience, I did begin to understand the role fear played in my current crisis. Fear prevented me from receiving the healing consolations that God, religion, and faith have to offer because it was *fear* that created the fire wall of anger that separated me from those things. Psychology teaches that once you've named it, you own it. Although the journey back to faith began with naming that which alienated me from God—fear and anger—it was a slow and gradual return, filled with moments of extreme doubt and, finally, unwavering certainty.

I have found more faith, and I feel that we rise to all occasions and are given special strengths to deal with special circumstances. Through Judith's [age 31] dying, I learned about the soul and the body and the relativity of time and even my own connection to what seems eternal. Gifted with this knowledge, I felt I had become an entirely different person. At first, this was freeing, but then, I did not know who I was, who I had been socialized to become all of my life and why I was even given my life. I had many ecstatic moments filled with the joy of feeling life itself. I also found myself in "the dark night of the soul," during the blacker, introspective circles of questioning. My sister's dying and death remains my life's most profound learning experience.

—ELISE, 36

While many surviving siblings experience the "dark night of the soul," as Elise describes above, others find the opposite to be true. In fact, some describe faith as the lifeline that connects them to the world, to God, and to their sibling. Grief makes us feel hopeless, helpless, and afraid; faith can counteract many of these feelings by nourishing our battered souls and fostering hope that we will somehow endure our loss.

In addition to the soothing and comforting aspects associated with faith, many surviving siblings feel as if their loss has actually enabled them to experience a deeper sense of wonder and spiritual awareness—an awareness that would not have been possible before their brother's or sister's death. Faith is often identified as the power responsible for enhancing one's spirituality which then both carries mourners through their loss and helps them find meaning in it. Of course, this spiritual growth usually does not happen immediately but over time, as the shock and pain begin to dissipate.

I do believe my faith has been a source of comfort. I believe that Sue [age 60] is with God and truly happy and at peace. I think Sue had very little happiness or peace in her lifetime. I also believe she is with me. I think loved ones are with you forever. This can't be explained, but I sometimes feel closer to those I've lost in death than I did in life. —JUDITH, 58

I feel I have grown spiritually after losing Kel [age 33] and other dear ones. I feel Kelly is in a better place, a place he is supposed to be at this point in time. I feel he watches over us and is with us. I feel we will all be together when we pass over. This belief has brought me peace of mind and made it easier to deal with other losses. —SEAN, 40

One of the ways faith is expressed externally is through religious affiliation. Many surviving siblings find strength in the familiar rituals and religious practices that have sustained them in the past. Religion can help connect us with others who have experienced suffering and loss in their own lives, both within our contemporary religious community and through the stories found in religious scriptures, like the Bible. These connections are really affirmations that our loss is significant, and those affirmations are often absent in cases of adult sibling bereavement.

My church family reached out to me through cards and food. They cried with me when I found out the tragic news that Ed [age 26] had been killed. People allowed me to talk about my grief and share stories about my brother, and they shared their stories of loss with me, too. —ANDREA, 31

Although I found it difficult to attend church for months after my brother's death, I slowly began to reshape my understanding of what it means to gather in God's name. For instance, before my brother's death, I'm ashamed to admit that I never thought much about the others who were in church with me—my friends, neighbors, and strangers who, like me, dragged themselves out of bed on a Sunday morning in search of something greater than themselves. I had always thought of church as my special time with God. But since my brother's death, I've gained a new appreciation for the community aspect of congregating.

I no longer see church as simply a time between God and me—after all, I don't have to go to church to experience oneness with God. Today, when I go to church, I look around at the community gathered in God's name—friends and neighbors who have problems with their teenagers, or who hate their jobs; people who have successful, happy lives, and those whose lives are plagued with sorrow and turmoil—and I think, "These are my sisters and brothers; we're one."

In many ways, religion gives a voice to grief; religious language helps us to grapple with the mysteries of the human condition, including the pain and separation of death. Of course, many religions offer the hope of eternal life, either in another realm (some call this otherworldly place heaven) or through rebirth into this world. This hope sustains and comforts mourners both in the knowledge that their brother or sister continues to exist and in the hope that they will be eventually be reunited with their sibling.

> *I hung on to my old Catholic belief in an afterlife. I know that I will see my brother Sean [age 45] again. I know that when I die, he will help me to the other side; he will be there.*
>
> —ROSEMARY, 51

> *I think that I'm more spiritual than before. I feel like one's soul cannot die, as it is a form of energy. I think we keep returning in new bodies and are smarter each time we return to this plane. I've met people I feel were/are old souls because of their wisdom and others who I think must be here for the first time.*
>
> —HARRI, 50

> *I like to think our brothers and sisters are watching over us and helping us through the tough times—like guardian angels. That's what I'd like to believe—but don't always.*
>
> —MARIE, 38

If attending religious services has been too painful since your sibling's death, you're not alone. Many mourners find religion and religious services ring hollow in the face of their loss.

Talk to me about the truth of religion and I'll listen gladly. Talk to me about the duty of religion and I'll listen submissively. But don't come talking to me about the consolations of religion or I shall suspect that you don't understand.

—C. S. LEWIS, *A Grief Observed*

Even members of the clergy confess that it's often difficult for the bereaved to feel connected to the rest of the congregation. Sermons and religious music often seem facile and superficial in the context of grief. This is understandable; after all, there are few things that can compare to the enormity of death. Sometimes it's just easier to stay home and avoid the situation altogether.

> *I believe that God took Lori [age 31] so she wouldn't suffer anymore. However, I have difficulty attending church. I was very involved with my church family in Dallas, but it's very difficult for me to attend now.* —DEBBIE, 37

> *Religion has generally been helpful; however, I've walked out of church a couple of times. "Amazing Grace" was very difficult to listen to and almost impossible to sing without crying.* —JAN, 56

One surviving sister told me, "I've been a Catholic all my life, but I now wonder if this is the right religion for me. I've been to church once since my brother died and it all felt like empty ritual. Maybe it's time for a change." The problem with this line of reasoning is that we may misinterpret a temporary aversion to religious services (a common grief response) as a rejection of our religion altogether. Of course, it's also fairly common to reshape religious attitudes following the death of a sibling, but only the passage of time will enable you to distinguish between the two. Remember, in early grief, it's often difficult to know just what you're feeling. This is why grief counselors advise the bereaved to refrain from making any major, life-altering decisions for at least a year following the death of a loved one. So, if you're unhappy with your religion and feel the need to experiment with other forms of religious expression, do so with caution.

Although religion is often identified as a positive, healing aspect of bereavement, this is not always the case. In fact, many surviving siblings either reject organized religion altogether or find that their religious affiliation made little or no difference with regard to their grief. Sometimes, religious attitudes can actually complicate grieving. For example, there are those who feel that expressing grief demonstrates a lack of faith; that if one professes a profound faith in God, this faith must naturally extend into the realm of loss. People who ascribe to this view understand grief as tantamount to an open expression of distrust in God. If this sounds incredible to you, think how often you've heard a bereaved person say something like this: "I know I shouldn't be sad right now because Jane is in a better place." Such a person has been taught that "real faith" renders one impervious to the pain of grief; that we should, in fact, rejoice when our loved one dies. The not-so-subtle message is that if you're unable to rejoice, then you must be a person of insufficient faith.

The truth is, grief is a healthy response to the death of a loved one, and repressed grief can lead to both psychological and physical problems. Grieving the loss of your brother or sister is first and foremost an expression of love—and love is the central virtue found in most religions. Further, repressing grief as a means of demonstrating one's religiosity stifles the community's response to console. Community support is usually considered an integral aspect of organized religion. Herman Melville wrote, "We cannot live only for ourselves. A thousand fibers connect us with our fellow humans." Grieving people need those connections more than ever. By hiding your grief, or maintaining a stiff upper lip for the sake of appearances, you deprive yourself of the healing love you will receive from others within your religious community.

If you've had trouble with religion in the past, either with a particular church's teaching, an individual member of the clergy, or any other issue that caused you to part ways with a particular religion, then your brother's or sister's death may actually reopen old wounds. Quite often, for one reason or another, the religion in which we were raised seems inadequate or unacceptable as we grow into adulthood. I often encounter students who harbor a great deal of resentment toward their parents for forcing religion upon them as children and not permitting them to have questions or opposing viewpoints. Consequently, many reject the religion of their childhood when they finally escape to college or beyond. For some, the scars of the past run deep, as Carol painfully describes.

I feel a great deal of anger in connection with Kathy's [age 34] death toward the Catholic Church, in which I was raised. I had rejected the church long before Kathy was diagnosed, because of the church's attitude toward abortion rights, homosexuality, and priestly celibacy. When Kathy died, I had new reasons for disgust and anger toward the church. When Kathy planned her wedding in 1982, the church told her that she could not have a church wedding because her fiancé was divorced. Yet, after she died, she was allowed a church memorial service in the Florida town where she lived briefly before she died, and a church funeral at my parents' parish church. When she needed the church, it rejected her; but when she was dead, it was right there. I find that revolting!

The priest at the memorial service had never met Kathy, but didn't admit that in his sermon. Instead, he seemed to read straight from "The Standard Funeral Sermon for a Young Person Unknown to the Priest." It was a lot of generic pabulum, and I resented that. But my anger at the church really boiled over when the priest at the next service, the funeral, started out by saying, "We are gathered here to celebrate . . ." I'd like to know what in the hell he thought he was celebrating! Kathy's ashes are now buried in a Catholic cemetery. I suppose that once you're dead, in the church's eyes, you're okay. —CAROL, 42

I believe that we're meant to ask questions; we're hardwired to seek the truth. The need to ask difficult questions, and the demand for answers, can become the driving force behind our grief journey. Of course, there are those who argue that to question God or to have doubts about religion is wrong, even sinful. But when we suppress the questions either because we're bullied into believing that we're bad people for questioning in the first place—or because we're afraid of the answers—then we run the risk of getting stuck in grief. Grief counselors refer to this as *complicated grief,* a condition that usually signals trouble. For example, failure to adequately address the questions and issues surrounding your sibling's death may lead to other problems. Future losses will be more difficult because the same questions are likely to surface with more urgency. And remember, with every new loss, we revisit past losses.

Socrates said, "An unexamined life is not worth living." When we engage in soul-searching and questioning, we push past our personal limitations and grow spiritually. Moreover, I believe that *God is there in the questioning.* In fact, God *encourages* the questioning. I often tell my students not to get too comfortable in their beliefs because beliefs are subject to change as life continues to unfold. In fact, I worry about the person who says, "I'm very comfortable with my beliefs, and I don't question my faith."

I've learned the hard way that life is change, and with change comes new ways of interpreting the world around us.

The answers to your questions will help you find meaning in your loss and probably reshape many of your beliefs. In the end, you may not believe many of the things you once held as truth before your brother or sister died, but if you've asked the questions and passed through the fires of doubt, then your spiritual life has probably deepened. Maybe you're able to appreciate the way in which God works through us and in us, sending others—family, friends, and even kind strangers—to help us through our sorrow. Or perhaps you've witnessed the courage of those who have painfully moved forward to rebuild their lives after devastating losses. People just like you and me.

> *I try to remember that she's only a veil away and that she's only around the corner, waiting for me. I want to bring my best to the time I have here, and there is a reason why I'm still here. My only choice is to go though this and come out on the other side. I try to think now about how blessed we always were . . . and still are. If this is the way it was going to go, there isn't one thing I would change about the time I shared with my sweet sister, Nora [age 33].* —KATHLEEN, 39

WHAT HELPS

Because the overwhelming majority of surviving siblings—and, indeed, most grieving people—wrestle with questions about faith and religion, the focus of this "What Helps" section is on helping both believers and nominal believers deal with what I have come to call *conflicts of the soul*.

First, I think it's important to reiterate that questions about faith, God, and religion are normal grief reactions. In fact, these questions are so commonplace that pastoral counselors call them *the questions of theodicy.* When used in this way, the term theodicy refers to the apparent disparity between the existence of a God who loves us and yet still permits evil (like suffering and grief) to enter our lives. Naturally, this paradox can lead to questions and doubts about faith.

> *I'm confused about God. I'm deeply disturbed that my brother was taken; he was such a beautiful human being! He never did anything wrong. Rob [age 35] lived life by the book, but in the end, it didn't do him any good.* —LISA, 33

The incomprehensibility of her brother's death leaves Lisa feeling bewildered and uncertain. Her brother was a good person who certainly didn't deserve to die at such a young age. His death naturally leads his sister to ask questions about God's fairness. Of course, there's nothing wrong with asking questions and having doubts. After all, questions and doubts indicate a level of mature faith; you must feel secure enough in your relationship with God to express doubts and to ask such questions in the first place. There are two ways to address such questions: through dialogue with others and through prayer.

Let's begin with dialogue. Your first task is perhaps the most challenging: find someone both capable and receptive to this type of dialogue. You might consider your grief partner, your best friend, your spouse, a sibling, or a member of the clergy—but just be certain the person you choose is close to your level of spiritual development. In other words, don't attempt to discuss questions about God's sovereignty and justice with someone who hasn't moved beyond their childhood understanding of faith and religion or you'll end up engaged in a negative confrontation that will leave you angry and frustrated. This means avoiding the narrow-minded, holier-than-thou types, too. If there's one thing I've learned in my many years of teaching religious studies, it's that those who profess to be holier-than-thou aren't. People of real faith don't need to spend time convincing the rest of us how holy they are.

If you're having difficulty finding someone with whom you can have an honest, heartfelt conversation about faith, you might consider pastoral counseling. Pastoral counselors are trained to help you sort out the complex issues of faith and religion in the context of grief. Most will offer practical suggestions to enable you to feel some sort of resolution (see "What Helps" in chapter 7). If all else fails, visit the Adult Sibling Grief website www.adultsiblinggrief.com). There you'll find others who both understand and sympathize with your conflicts, questions, and doubts.

> *I have received the comfort of caring and supportive ministers, both from my own church and my family's home church as well. I believe that Paul [age 48] is in a place of rest and peace and that he will no longer be plagued by whatever loneliness or unhappiness he was feeling.*
> —L. B., 55

My second suggestion is simple: pray. And pray like you mean it, even if your heart isn't in it. This may sound as if I'm advocating false prayer; on the contrary, I happen to believe that prayer is a powerful energy that not only puts us in touch with God, but with ourselves and others. If you're struggling with faith and religion right now, this may not seem like a very helpful suggestion. "Why should I pray when I'm not sure what I believe anymore?" is a legitimate question. Beyond the touted religious aspects of prayer is another important feature often overlooked by those who demur at the practice. The truth is, prayer has a profound psychological dimension. I remember reading that the renowned psychiatrist Carl Jung often recommended prayer to his patients. The power of prayer is often found in the calming effect it has on those who pray. Moreover, prayer can help to put you in touch with the essence of your conflicts about faith and religion. Once you understand what it is that separates you from God, you'll be in a better position to deal with it.

But if you're either unable to pray or hesitant to try, perhaps you need to change the way in which you approach prayer. I found that my old way of praying simply didn't work for me after my brother died. In fact, for a long time, I couldn't pray at all. Finally, rather than abandon the practice of prayer altogether, I experimented with different ways of praying until I found a new way to reach out to God. Today, my prayers are a mixture of conversation and gratitude—far different from the rote prayers I'd learned as a child and practiced into adulthood.

> *I couldn't pray for a long time after Nora [age 33] died. I still really don't know how to pray anymore—or I pray differently. My prayers no longer ask for outcomes. I try to pray that whatever happens, I, or the person being prayed for, can handle what comes their way.* —KATHLEEN, 39

In order for prayer to be successful, you'll first need to commit yourself to the idea that prayer can be a helpful and healing resource. Here are several steps you can take to enhance your prayer experience.

- Set aside time—as little as five minutes per day—specifically for prayer.
- Pray in a quiet, comfortable, room that is free from distractions.
- As far as what to say or how to say it, pray in whatever way feels most comfortable for you, but pray as if you believe God is listening.
- Think of prayer as an ongoing dialogue with God; this means that you don't have to lay out all of your questions and problems in one sitting. In fact, it's best to narrow your focus rather than pray in generalities.

If you're unaccustomed to prayer and don't know where to begin, you might consider reading one or all of the following:

- Don M. Aycock's *Prayer 101: What It Is, What It Isn't, How to Do It* is a short book, but it's filled with helpful suggestions to get you started.
- Don Postema's *Space for God: The Study and Practice of Prayer and Spirituality* combines prayer and art into an inspiring book that will help to quiet your soul and ease you into a contemplative mood.
- *The Power of Prayer Around the World*, by Glenn Mosley and Joanna Hill, celebrates the diversity of faiths and prayer experiences. This is a wonderful book that offers how-to information on a variety of prayerful expressions.
- *The Bible.* Praying with the Bible, particularly the psalms, is always a moving experience, and chances are that you probably already have a Bible on your shelf. I remember reading Psalm 22 over and over again and feeling a great deal of consolation in connecting with the ancient writer who, like me, cried out against the injustice of undeserved suffering to a God who seemed so far away.

> *My God, my God, why have you abandoned*
> *me?*
> *Why so far from my call for help,*
> *from my cries of anguish?*
> *My God, I call by day, but you do not answer;*
> *by night, but I have no relief.*
> —PS. 22:1–3

Both prayer and dialogue with others can help reduce the anxiety associated with conflicts of the soul. I've mentioned the importance of asking questions and searching for the truth. And truth can be found not only in religion, but also in books, in our own experiences, and in stories and advice from others. Perhaps most important, the search for truth is essentially a search for meaning. Finding meaning in our loss enables us to incorporate it into our lives and to heal.

> *When Forest drowned, I was 23 and he was 18. He and our other brother went rafting on Easter Sunday, and the river was swollen with snowmelt. They came upon a waterfall, where Forest was pinned underneath and drowned. This was the first profound loss of my life. I missed the future we lost. I don't know why, but learning to grieve became the most important thing I did for a year. I read books, heard Dr. Elisabeth Kübler-Ross speak, and took a class on grieving. I allowed myself to feel. Looking back, learning to grieve honored Forest's life and prepared me for other losses.* —ANN, 47

> *I found two books especially helpful:* The Courage to Grieve, *by Judy Tatelbaum, and* Praying Our Goodbyes, *by Joyce Rupp, OSM. Both authors are bereaved siblings. During the first couple of years, I read anything and everything about death, grief, and sibling loss that I could get my hands on. Listening to the painful stories of others helped me to have the courage and hope to live the rest of my life.* —JULIE, 37

· · ·

After my brother's death, I questioned God's fairness and even doubted God's existence for the first time in my life. There were times when I shook my fist and railed at the heavens, and days when the stranglehold of fear held my soul prisoner, demanding from God as ransom the answers to the weighty questions about life and death I could not find in my fancy theology textbooks. There were terrible days when I could not forgive God for betraying me or forgive myself for feeling betrayed. All those moments, and many more, are forever seared into my memory, woven into my own unique tapestry of grief. And through it all—the fear, the anger, the questions, the doubts, and the river of tears—was God. I know this for one reason and one reason alone: I survived.

Although you may not believe it now, you, too, will survive this unimaginable loss. You may be confused about faith, God, and religion, and you might legitimately wonder if these things have a place in your life any longer. Perhaps you're feeling alienated from God—or angry at God for allowing such heartache to enter your life. You may wonder if you'll ever have your life back, if you'll ever be truly happy again, if you'll ever stop feeling afraid, if you'll ever be able to trust God again. The answer to these and many other questions will come only with the passage of time; therefore, be kind to yourself and patient in the waiting. You don't need to rationalize or apologize for any of the feelings associated with grief—even negative feelings directed at God.

Whether your sojourn of grief is presently marked by days or decades, remember that you do not travel alone. God's healing light penetrates the darkness of despair in countless forms—your near and dear ones, friends, coworkers, and, most especially, other surviving siblings who are with you in spirit as you move forward on your journey of loss. I wish I could promise that your grief will come to an end; it does not. But it will get better. With each passing day, you'll continue to miss your brother or sister, but the lifetime of love you've shared forever binds you together in that special way only siblings can know and understand. This love, and the enduring love of God, will empower you to learn to live again in a world without your beloved sibling.

10

ACCEPTANCE

A Search for Meaning

So, we'll go no more a roving
So late into the night,
Though the heart be still as loving
And the moon be still as bright.

—LORD BYRON

AFEW months after my brother died, things begin to get a little fishy. It starts with a dream so vivid and detailed, that for several days I can't get the images out of my head. In the dream, my sister Linda and I are waiting in a restaurant lounge. The restaurant, obviously Italian, is lavishly furnished with ornate red velvet chairs, and the walls are adorned with paintings in gilded frames. We wait for quite awhile and then, much to our collective joy, our brother enters the room and tells us to follow him. Linda and I are very excited to see him, but neither of us wants to spoil the evening by mentioning the fact that we thought he was dead, so we try to act very casual about the whole thing.

My brother leads us down a long hallway into a private banquet room where a party is apparently already under way. Seated around the table are several deceased relatives, including my grandfather, my beloved aunt Camella and uncle John, and many others. I'm very happy to see them all again, alive and having a wonderful time. Linda and I take our place at the end of the table and look on, smiling, as the people we'd loved so much in life are now laughing, eating, and drinking wine as they always had. Strangely, none of them take notice of Linda and me, but neither of us feels particularly bothered by this.

My brother seems to be the host of this little party; he walks around the table chatting with the guests and serving them food. Oddly, the only menu option seems to be fish. As I scan the table, I see huge platters brimming with every conceivable type of fish—but nothing else. This presents a problem for me because I don't eat fish. I turn to my sister and whisper, "What am I going to eat? There's nothing here but fish!" Before she can answer, my brother, suddenly standing beside my chair, bends down and asks, "Aren't you going to eat anything?" I don't want to hurt his feelings—he seems so happy and proud at the way the party is going—but I finally tell him, "There's nothing here for me to eat." He smiles, as if suddenly remembering how much I hate fish. "Don't worry," he says. "I'm going to go and find something else for you to eat. I'll be back in a little while."

And then the dream ends.

The next day, I'm still puzzling over the meaning of the fish dream when one of my students approaches me after class and shyly hands me a small box. "What's this? I ask, surprised. She smiles and says, "It's a good-bye gift." (I had recently accepted a new position at the university where I presently teach and had announced my resignation to the students a few days before.) "I made it myself," she tells me as I untie the ribbon. I open the box and nearly fall over. Inside is a delicate pair of earrings: tiny, silvery-white fish dangling on gold hooks.

Driving home that afternoon, thinking it peculiar that I should receive the fish earrings after my dream the night before, I suddenly remember that the first dream I'd had about my brother after his death *also* included fish. (In that particular dream, we were eating Swedish Fish candy.) As I try to make sense of all this fishiness, I wonder if perhaps my brother is trying to communicate with me. I feel a little silly even thinking along these lines, but what else could it be? Later that evening, I decide to share my "fish tales" with my husband. He listens thoughtfully, and then asks me a question that seems to solve the puzzle: "Isn't the fish a religious symbol?"

Of course! That has to be it! I had been engaged in a titanic struggle with God, faith, and religion ever since my brother died. Perhaps the fish symbol that appeared in my dreams is somehow

connected to that. I explain to my husband that the fish, originally a pagan religious symbol, was adopted by early Christians
(who, at the time, were being persecuted) as a way to recognize
one another; sort of like a password. The Greek word for fish,
ichthys, was used acrostically; that is, each of the letters stood for
something (*Iesous Christos Theou Yios Soter*, which means Jesus
Christ, Son of God, Savior). In later times, fish were associated
with several gospel stories (for example, Jesus multiplying loaves
and fishes and Jesus calling on his disciples to be "fishers of
men").

As far as the student who gave me the earrings, she would
have understood the fish symbol from taking my class.

It all makes perfect sense. I feel a great deal of satisfaction in
having apparently solved the fish mystery—but days later, my
seemingly astute connections would be abandoned and replaced
by a meaning so profound that it literally changed the course of
my grief journey.

My brother's final request was that his ashes be distributed
in the Gulf of Mexico and that this be done in the spring. So, in
late May, my family gathers on a secluded little stretch of beach
just off Longboat Key, to honor my brother's last wishes. We
wait until just before sunset and then, after holding a little
prayer service, swim out to a sandbar with his ashes. As I swim,
I talk to my brother. "I never thought I'd have to go through life
without you and there are times when I don't have the courage
to face another day. If there's any way you can help me learn
how to live again, I'd be grateful." I start to sob then, and lag
behind the others, who have nearly reached the sandbar. I stop
swimming and tread water for a moment, watching the sun as it
lazily sinks just below the horizon. And then, something amazing happens: A large, silvery-white fish leaps out of the water
and brushes lightly against my shoulder before disappearing
into the depths.

In that instant, time seems to stand still. The events leading up to this moment coalesce into perfect meaning. The fish: appearing first as the sweet candy of the past, then as the dinner I refused to eat, prompting my brother's search and promise to return "in a little while," followed by the handmade farewell gift, which symbolized letting go of the past and moving on to a new adventure—and now, one final fish, this one alive and free in the unseen realm beneath these still waters. In one euphoric instant, the universe makes sense; my tears are replaced with laughter.

I swim furiously toward the sandbar, renewed in spirit, and, along with those who loved my brother most, cast his ashes into the sea.

• • •

The experience of that day in the waters off the coast of Florida has truly changed my life. Whether the fish connections were merely coincidental or something more mysterious, I'll never know with certainty; but one thing I do know is that after that day, I began to accept my brother's death.

But what *is* acceptance? When some of the grief experts speak of acceptance, or *resolution*, they usually mean that the mourner has in some way been released from an emotional attachment to the deceased. But this definition does not reflect my understanding of acceptance. In fact, I don't think it's possible to *detach* from our sibling. After all, we're bonded through love, and love is eternal; it cannot be extinguished, even by death. Acceptance, to me, involves learning to live again through finding meaning in your loss and then incorporating your loss into your life. But not everyone agrees with this particular perspective. In fact, some surviving siblings reject the whole idea of acceptance.

To me, acceptance means that I'm okay with Dana's [age 21] death. I'm not! Oh, I know she is dead. But I'm not comfortable with it. Acceptance, to me, means that I'm letting her go. I can't do that. I don't want to do that. My grief is my only connection to her. —RONNA, 34

My younger sister, Mary-Lee [age 28], was accidentally killed almost twenty-eight years ago. I don't believe I've ever accepted her death. I know I'll never see her or hear her voice again— never laugh with her or chitchat with her or argue with her ever again. On this level, I accept her death. At the same time, though, I can't accept the tremendous loss to all who would have known her had she lived. —MARYLIN, 65

But how and when does the process of acceptance begin? Generally speaking, you'll probably notice some subtle changes in your grieving. The grief spasms will become less frequent, you'll begin to have moments, and then longer periods of time, when you're not actively mourning. And you'll probably experience fewer episodes of anger and depression; you'll begin to feel better about yourself and feel more in control of things. All of this happens so slowly that many of the changes are, at first, imperceptible, but, in reality, you've been moving in the direction of acceptance all along.

As time passed, there were longer and longer periods of time in which I wasn't totally consumed with his death. Eventually, I reached the point where the time that I was not thinking about him became greater than the time when I was thinking about him. I still cry sometimes, but it's not a devastating, sickening feeling anymore. It's more like an emptiness or a tugging of the heartstrings. —LISA-MARIE, 34

I think I began to accept Stefani's [age 25] death about two years after she died. Although I didn't think it would ever be possible, the rawness of the pain of losing Stefani decreased significantly after the second year. It was, and still is, painful to think of her dying and of losing her, but after the second year, the waves of acute pain became much less severe and much more spread apart. After the third year, I felt more comfortable managing my feelings of loss. —DEAN, 30

In the beginning, grief is like walking barefoot on glass: every day, every moment is acutely painful. Over time, however, the intensity of grief subsides and is usually replaced by a longing of sorts. Finally, most surviving siblings emerge from the seemingly solitary world of early grief as changed persons. Of course, the grief never really goes away, but the periods of acute grief and longing diminish greatly.

Lots of people think that there is a timetable for "getting over" a death like this, but I don't think it's something you actually "get over." The best analogy I have come up with is that it's like a giant hole that suddenly and inexplicably appears in your living room floor. You couldn't prevent it from happening, and for the rest of your life you will wish it weren't there, that your living room was like it used to be, like everyone else's. At first, you will fall into that big hole constantly, because it's so new and unavoidable. But, as you live with it longer, it doesn't get any smaller; you just sort of get used to it being there. Sometimes you still fall into it, but generally not as often, and each time it gets a bit easier to get back out. And sometimes you will choose to climb down in the hole for a while, because you need to, and then you'll climb out again when you're ready. But if you try to deny the hole is there, or believe that it will somehow go away, you'll hurt even more. —JULIANNE, 40

I don't think you ever accept the death of a sibling; you just try to learn how to carry on day by day with the loss.
—MARIE, 38

Julianne describes a steady move toward acceptance without denying the fact that her sibling's death will always remain an ever-present reality. And although your movement forward may be marked by small steps, there are certain moments—I call them *pivotal events*—that may occur along the way that aid in the process of acceptance. For example, I consider the "fish experience" a pivotal event because it helped me to understand that my brother is still very much a part of my life, even though he's physically no longer here.

Frank's story demonstrates how a pivotal event changed both his perception of his brother and the meaning of his death.

When I saw Marshall's [age 46] death certificate, I noticed that "chronic obstructive lung disease" was listed as a "complication." The actual cause of death was given as "accident." What kind of accident? And who and what caused it? I talked to his physicians, examined the medical history, and learned that the autopsy revealed three times the lethal dose of his medication, theophylline, in his bloodstream. I could find no evidence of medical malfeasance among the hospital personnel, although it was possible. The fact is, he was dying and he knew it. Each incidence of being rushed to the emergency room, unable to breathe, must have been horrendous for him, much as his childhood asthmatic seizures must have been. About a month later, late at night, I broke into a crying jag as it suddenly became clear to me that Marshall, sick and tired of being sick and tired (literally!), bedridden and helpless, probably had hastened the inevitable, willfully. Marshall had not been one to take responsibility for his life. That he would, in the end, assume this last possible measure somehow comforted me. It still does. I would like to think that given his circumstances, I would do much the same thing. I called a friend of mine in Chicago and spoke of my thoughts, all the while being able to vent my feelings. I felt better after that, and the healing process started. —FRANK, 52

About a year after my brother's death, I read Sarah Ban Breathnach's book *Simple Abundance* and decided to include gratitude as part of my grief journal. As I wrote about all the obvious things for which I'm grateful (my husband, children, family, friends, dogs, and career) it suddenly occurred to me that despite all the suffering and grief of the past year, I'd do it all over again. I realized that even though losing my brother was a terrible event, given the choice, I wouldn't have missed the chance to be his sister, even if I knew things would end this way. Although this realization wasn't as dramatic as the fish event, it was nonetheless a pivotal moment. I began to let go of the anger and sense of betrayal I still felt at God and the universe for the awful suffering inflicted upon my family and me. I remember actually feeling lighter and, yes, happier, as if a huge weight had been lifted off my shoulders.

> *It was at least a year after Lois [age 30] died, but I remember specifically one day realizing that I was more grateful for the thirty years she lived rather than feeling so terribly unhappy that she died so young. From then on, whenever I found myself starting to feel so sad, I'd remind myself to think about the good times and feel happy about them.* —RAE ELLEN, 53

Acceptance usually happens once we've attached meaning to our loss. This meaning may include such things as personal growth or spiritual awakening and will be different for each of us. We may begin to see new connections and interpret certain events in new and meaningful ways. For example, psychiatrist Viktor Frankl (*Man's Search for Meaning*) tells the story of a widower who, after two years, was unable to move forward in his grief journey; the death of his wife was simply too much for him to bear, and so he remained stuck in depression. According to Frankl, the widower eventually found meaning in his loss by realizing that had he died first, *she* would be the one suffering instead of him; he had, in fact, spared her the pain of grief by surviving her. This gave meaning to the widower's suffering.

Bereavement author Thomas Attig speaks of a "transition from loving in presence to loving in absence." I've made this transition; after five years, I've adjusted to my brother's *physical* absence. I know that I can't pick up the phone and call him anymore, and I know that he's never going to see my children grow up; we'll never take another long walk on the beach together, and we'll never take that trip to Israel, as we had planned.

This adjustment usually begins when we ask the eternal question: Why? Why did my sibling have to die in the first place? In asking this question, we begin the search for meaning. For most surviving siblings, attaching a particular meaning to their loss helps them to move forward and begin rebuilding their lives. For me, the senseless tragedy of my brother's passing takes on new meaning in many ways; I begin to see my brother's death as personally transforming. For example, losing my brother has taught me to embrace life in a more dynamic and passionate way, and I care less about what others think and more about what seems right for me. And I'm no longer afraid of death because I'm secure in my belief that death is not the end, but merely a transition. There have been many other changes as well, but I doubt that any of these changes would have taken place had I not been forced into the sustained period of contemplation and self-reflection brought about by my brother's death.

> *I realize that life is short, in the span of "forever," whether one dies in childhood or at age one hundred. I've learned that things and stuff are not that important. Our legacy at death is the people whom we touch along the way. This has helped me accept Gail's [age 40] absence. It has also made me try to focus more on the present—today—because tomorrow may not come, and yesterday is over.* —HARRI, 50

. . .

Fall came early the year my brother died. The leaves gave hints of change as early as August, and by late September, I began the Leaf War. But the leaves fell faster than I could rake them. I worked diligently, gathering them into great piles, only to have the wind, obviously on the side of the leaves, blow them around the yard again. After a few days, the battle seemed futile, so I surrendered, leaving a scattered mound of leaves in the middle of the front yard, a monument to my defeat.

My children and a few of their friends decided I'd created the leaf pile for their enjoyment. I stood on the front steps, watching them jump in and out of the heap, tossing leaves above their heads. Even a scruffy neighborhood dog joined in the fun. As I turned to go into the house, something made me freeze in my tracks. Mingled with the laughter of the other children was my brother's distinctive laughter—I'd know it anywhere. I turned around, half-expecting to see him—and there it was again, my brother's laugh. My brother wasn't there that day, of course, but his nephew was. As it turns out, my older son has my brother's laugh, but I never recognized it before that fall afternoon.

That was nearly five years ago, and although I felt a surge of grief then, today, whenever I hear my nearly grown son laugh, I think of my brother and smile. My brother's laughter lives on in my son, and I feel grateful for the connection. And there are other connections, too. I've begun to notice things I've never noticed before: My niece, Dena, has my brother's blue eyes; my daughter, Annie, has his wicked sense of humor; and my son Jack has his unique and spontaneous kindness. These connections are not so much reminders of what I've lost, but of my brother's enduring gifts—gifts that continue to live on in the people we both love and treasure.

I have managed, in some ways, to incorporate Nancy [age 40] into my own life, in a way that is comforting to me. One thing Nancy and I share, despite our twelve-year age difference, is our voice. On the telephone, even our parents could not tell us apart. Right after Nancy died, this was a problem. I called my mother and she began to cry, saying, "I thought you were her." But now, when I'm talking, sometimes I'll hear her in my voice and feel as though she's with me. I also find myself making a face or a gesture that will remind me of Nancy. This reminds me how much she played a part in my identity, and still does.

—J. ELIZABETH, 31

Over time, I began to take comfort in other things that may have, in the past, triggered tears. For example, the photographs of my brother I took down and placed in a box after his death are now displayed around my house. One rests on my computer monitor as a source of hope and encouragement on those days when I feel tired or frustrated. I'm now able to tell funny stories about him without crying, and I feel his gentle, loving presence as I struggle to become a better person. He, more than anyone else I've ever known, was able to appreciate the innate goodness in others. Each time I'm able to accept someone as they are, each time I'm able to love without condition, I continue his legacy of compassion.

Acceptance seemed to begin about four years after James's [age 29] death, when I realized that I would rather remember him every day with tears than go one day without thinking about him at all. I started remembering the times we had together, like the night out shortly before he died. I had never felt closer to him. And I finally did accept that he is in a better place. It's still difficult to write or talk about it without getting tears in my eyes, but that's okay. It shows that the love is still in my heart and I haven't grown cold.   —NADINE, 41

My brother's death has shown me that grief mirrors life. In the beginning, we're helpless; we must rely on others to care for us. Soon there are some things we can do on our own, but we're still needy; we make mistakes, and sometimes we feel frustrated, angry, depressed, and overwhelmed by our inability to do certain things that people further along are able to do. Eventually, we grow up. We learn that life is a mixture of good and bad, joy and sorrow, and that most of the time, life proceeds on a fairly even keel. Sure, there may be obstacles and difficulties along the way, but we've learned how to deal with most of life's challenges. And so it is with acceptance. As the shock and hopelessness of those early weeks and months eventually subsides, ever so slowly, we begin to heal through the meaning we find in our loss.

Of course, finding meaning doesn't mean the grief magically disappears. For me, the grief is still present, incorporated into the person I've become as a result of my brother's passing. It has evolved into a shadowy companion that always walks a step behind. At any given moment, I can turn and face the shadow, and sometimes the shadow demands attention. But most days now, the shadow remains silent—yet forever just a step away.

> *After five years, I finally feel like Michael's absence isn't as acutely and constantly agonizing now. I feel more absorbed in the love we shared, rather than feeling completely ripped-off of our adult lives together. I feel more peaceful as I continue to miss him every day.*
> —HEIDI, 34

WHAT HELPS

A few weeks after my brother died, a neighbor told me, "Time heals all wounds." At the time, consumed with sorrow, I thought her comment superficial and not at all comforting. But now I understand that more than anything else, the passage of time has helped soothe the sting of my brother's death.

> *Although the support of friends and family helped during the grieving process, I truly feel that time was the most significant factor in my coming to some level of healing and peace.*
>
> —DEAN, 30

While it's true that time does heal, the fact remains that when you're grieving, it's difficult to imagine you'll ever feel normal again. During that first year after my brother's death, I often felt discouraged and frustrated at my inability to move forward. Grief, for me, was very much a two steps forward, one step backward journey. At some point, however, things changed. I began to search for and then eventually found meaning in both my brother's death and in my own suffering; this is how I eventually learned to accept his death.

The search for meaning is usually a spontaneous outgrowth of grief that occurs over time. Moreover, the meaning we attach to our sibling's death will be different for each of us. Of course, if you're still grappling with the senselessness of your brother's or sister's death, you may find it difficult to even consider searching for meaning. In fact, you might feel that this almost trivializes your loss. If this is the case, you may not be ready to continue with this process. Put this chapter aside and return to it at a later date.

If, however, you feel as though your brother's or sister's death has changed you and caused you to reevaluate your priorities, or if you feel as though there's some greater purpose to your suffering, then you're probably ready to move forward. What follows are several examples of how other surviving siblings searched for and then found meaning in their loss. Helpful suggestions designed to initiate your own search for meaning are also included.

There seem to be two very general categories of meaning-making activities: remembering and the call-to-action.

In early grief, remembering can be a painful process. Simply talking about your sibling in the past tense, for example, can instigate tears and feelings of profound loss. Over time, however, remembering usually brings comfort and helps us to remain connected to our sibling. The most common way bereaved siblings remember is through storytelling. Storytelling helps to keep memories alive, allows us to relive special moments with our brother or sister, and to share those moments with others.

Perhaps most important, storytelling allows us to remember those qualities about our sibling we loved most dearly; many times, we're able to see those cherished traits reflected back in ourselves. For instance, when I tell stories about my brother, I find that most of them include anecdotes about his contagious sense of humor or his quiet patience. When I see these characteristics reflected back in myself or those I love, I feel as if he's still a part of my life in a very profound and meaningful way.

> *I literally feel as if I have gained some of Judith's [age 31] personality, and I feel lucky to have absorbed her best quality: her absolute integrity.* —ELISE, 36

In addition to storytelling, there are other remembering activities that can aid in meaning making. One such activity is the creation of a sibling scrapbook. A sibling scrapbook should highlight and celebrate the special relationship you shared with your sibling and differs from the sibling storybook discussed in chapter 6 (although both can be helpful meaning-making activities). The sibling scrapbook should span the whole of your brother's or sister's life; think of it as a history. This holistic approach will allow you to view the totality of your brother's or sister's life and to recognize the important role you played in it. After all, you were there from the beginning; you were there through the skinned knees, the adolescent turmoil, and the transition into adulthood. No one else can claim this special place in the history shared by you and your sibling.

Try not to be too intimidated by the actual process of putting the scrapbook together. Scrapbook making is quite popular today, and for those of us who can't tell the difference between a glue stick and a carrot stick, rest assured, there's a variety of resources available to get you started (see "Chapter Resources" in the appendix).

Martha took the scrapbook idea one step further and decided to construct a family memory book about her sister Paula. In order to make the memory book even more meaningful and special, she involved family and friends.

> *After Paula's death, I knew I had to do something to record what our family meant to each other. I came up with a short letter and sent it to forty relatives and close family friends, asking for their reminiscences, ideas, quips, stories, and pictures for a book I would produce. Losing Paula [age 59] made me consider that it could be any of us in her place, and I didn't want the story that is our family to go unwritten. So far, I've received fifteen responses. I plan to put the book together this summer and distribute it at a family gathering on Thanksgiving weekend.*
>
> —MARTHA, 46

If scrapbooks aren't your style, you might consider creating a video memorial instead. A video memorial combines photographs, home videos, and other memorabilia into a lasting tribute to your sibling. Most videos are also set to music of your choosing. There are several computer-based programs, such as Personal Author, that enable you to combine words, photos, sound, slides, and film into a unique and lasting memorial. If you're not up to the challenge of creating a video yourself, you can have a professional do this for you (see "Chapter Resources" in the appendix).

Storytelling, scrapbooks, and video memorials are all creative ways to help us to remember our sibling and his or her special place within the greater circle of family and friends. As we tell stories about them or work to create a lasting memorial, we're likely to reinterpret certain events in light of our brother's or sister's death. For example, I was forever advising my brother to slow down as he traveled and moved around from place to place. He had many friends and always seemed to be on the go, eager to experience all that life had to offer. I now find a great deal of meaning in looking at the old postcards and photographs he sent me from exotic places; I remember him now and think, "He sure crammed a lot of living into those forty-three years." This, of course, in no way diminishes his passing, but it does help me feel better knowing that he enjoyed his life and was able to fulfill many of his dreams.

The second way many surviving siblings find meaning in their loss is by viewing their sibling's death as a call to action. For instance, championing a particular cause, such as training for and then running in a marathon to benefit breast cancer research, can help us to understand our loss in a larger context. That is, perhaps our own tragedy will enable us to help others and may even prevent others from enduring the type of suffering and loss we've had to bear.

> *After surviving this tragedy, I decided to become a bereavement therapist. I completed my master's in social work this year and have worked with many bereaved children and adults.*
>
> —VICTORIA, 26

Darcey found meaning in Donna's death through her involvement in a public awareness campaign designed to educate others about the potential dangers present in many national parks. She assumed a leadership role in both disseminating information and in moving forth with litigation.

> *Taking an active role somehow made me accept Donna's [age 38] death and the circumstances surrounding her death. I made memorial crosses [to remember the eight people who perished along with Donna in this terrible accident] that soon became sort of an icon of this tragic event. I started to reconstruct the events that occurred though my contact with the other families of those injured in the accident. I finally found a law firm that would represent the families in this event, and about twenty or so lawsuits will now be filed. None of us are doing this for the money. We just want to make sure that our loved ones did not suffer and die in vain. Hawaii attracts tourists from all over the world, and I want to make sure that no one suffers the same fate that Donna and the others did. I want to make sure that our parks and our hiking trails are safe for everyone. I created a website that allowed me to start sharing the truth about the events that day and the history of tragic events that happened in that particular park. The Learning Channel found my website. Although I'm forever sad about never seeing Donna again, I am pleased that my efforts started a documentary for others to learn, feel, and know.* —DARCEY, 37

Betty, on the other hand, understands Bill's death as a sort of wake-up call to pursue her life's passion. Here she describes how Bill's death inspired her to move forward with her research and writing. Notice how she's able to attach meaning to her work through acknowledging Bill's pride in her accomplishment as the driving force behind her efforts.

> *Accepting Bill's [age 76] death began with writing a novel. Then, simply following my interests, I became a researcher of*

church history. While my health did not permit the education to become a church historian in the academic sense, my physical limitations did allow the reading and research necessary to complete a manuscript on the history of the priesthood. I feel that Bill would be proud that I've become a church historian.

—BETTY, 75

What has allowed me to accept Judith's [age 31] death is the great knowledge this whole event has bestowed upon me. I don't think of her as gone: She is now partly within me and partly within all things, having dispersed her spirit. She is with me and she is gone; together, all at once. —ELISE, 36

Like Victoria, Darcey, and Betty, I, too, have come to understand my sibling's death as a call-to-action. Although much of that first terrible year following my brother's death seems hazy and unreal—I often refer to it as "the year I spent in a coma"—I slowly came to the conclusion that surviving adult siblings are indeed the *forgotten bereaved*, and I resolved to do something about it. As I moved forward on my journey, each time I tried to find information about adult sibling grief and found nothing, each time my loss was dismissed as insignificant, each time I had the opportunity to speak with other surviving siblings who felt similarly, I would think, "Someone ought to write a book on this subject." Although I never thought that I myself would be the one to write such a book, I soon realized that only someone who had experienced the loss of an adult sibling could do justice to the subject.

This project, and the countless surviving siblings who so generously shared their stories with me, have not only given great meaning to my own loss, they have also taught me some enduring lessons. I've learned that even though the world seems harsh and unforgiving at times, it is also filled with tremendous love. After all, you can't experience profound grief if you haven't first experienced profound love. And even though I often *felt* abandoned and alone in my grief, I know now that I was not. There were certain special people—family, friends, colleagues, neighbors, and sometimes even complete strangers—who reached out and supported me when I needed it the most. I am both grateful and humbled by this realization. I also like to think that my brother himself played a large part in walking me through the darkest moments as I struggled to find meaning in his passing and to rebuild my life.

I've already mentioned that I'm not the same person I was before I lost my brother. I'm a little wiser, a little more compassionate, a little bit tougher. But I'm glad for these changes because they remind me of the journey that brought me to this place—this place of acceptance and, finally, peace.

APPENDIX

Chapter Resources

1. SHOCK: DEALING WITH THE NEWS

Frankl, Viktor. *Man's Search for Meaning*. New York: Washington Square Press, 1998.

Kübler-Ross, Elisabeth. *On Death and Dying*. New York: Macmillan, 1969.

2. DENIAL: THIS CAN'T BE HAPPENING!

For help in planning a funeral, contact
National Funeral Directors Association
11121 W. Oklahoma Ave.
Milwaukee, WI 53227
(414) 541-2500
http://www.nfda.org/mediacenter/nfdafact.html

To purchase fabric for funeral crepe/bunting, contact
Victoria Louise Mercers
P.O. Box 266
Jefferson, MD 21755
(301) 473-4949
http://www.victorialouise.com

To order an external symbol of mourning, contact
My Heart's Missing Link
P.O. Box 0992
Allen Park, MI 48101
http://www.myheartsmissinglink.com

My Heart's Missing Link makes heart-shaped pendants (with a missing link and your sibling's birthstone in the center) to wear as an external symbol of mourning and loss.

3. THE REACTIONS OF OTHERS: WHY CAN'T YOU UNDERSTAND?

Frankl, Viktor. *Man's Search for Meaning*. New York: Washington Square Press, 1998.

4. SEARCHING FOR SOLITUDE: TO GO WITHIN

Attig, Thomas. *How We Grieve: Relearning the World*. New York: Oxford University Press, 1996.

Bowlby, John. *Attachment and Loss*. Vols. 1–2. New York: Basic Books, 1969–1973. Vol. 3. London: Hogarth Press, 1980.

Music

All musical selections are available at http://www.amazon.com.

For additional resources, visit http://www.growingthroughgrief. com. This website is dedicated to the emotional healing of the bereaved through music and a series of audio recordings designed to help mourners rebuild their lives after a loss. Ordering information is available at the site.

Aromatherapy

Davis, Patricia. *Aromatherapy: An A–Z*. Essex, UK: C. W. Daniel, 1996. For a good introduction to aromatherapy, visit http://www.aromamarket.com. And for information as well as products for purchase, http://www.aromaweb.com is an excellent site.

5. ANGER: HOW DARE THIS HAPPEN!

For help in learning yoga or the art of meditation, see:

Christensen, Alice. *The American Yoga Association's Beginner's Manual*. New York: Fireside, 2002.

Roche, Lorin. *Meditation Made Easy*. San Francisco: HarperCollins, 1998.

Herbal Remedies

Castleman, Michael. *The Healing Herbs: The Ultimate Guide to the Curative Power of Nature's Medicines*. New York: Rodale, 1991.

For information on herbal supplements, see http://www.holistic online.com/herbal-med/hol herb.htm or http://www.herbaladvi sor.com.

6. Guilt, Regret, Conflicts:
Shoulda, Coulda, Woulda

For help in creating a memory quilt, see:

Bonsib, Sandy. *Quilting Your Memories: Inspirations for Designing with Image Transfers.* Woodinville, Wash.: Martingale & Co., 1999.

Zieman, Nancy. *10–20–30 Minutes to Quilt.* Birmingham, Ala.: Oxmoor House, 2000.

For quilting instruction and supplies, see:

http://www.denverfabrics.com.

7. Depression: How Low Can You Go?

Wolfelt, Alan D. *Death and Grief: A Guide for Clergy and Others Involved in Care of the Bereaved.* Muncie, Ind.: Accelerated Development, 1988. Although the title implies that this is a book for clergy, it's an excellent resource for anyone who has suffered the loss of a loved one. I particularly like Wolfelt's discussion on depression insofar as it relates to grief.

Wright, Jesse H. and Monica Ramirez Basco. *Getting Your Life Back: The Complete Guide to Recovery from Depression.* New York: Free Press, 2001. There are literally hundreds of books about depression, but I found this one to be unique in its approach because it not only describes depression in easy to understand terms, it offers practical steps in helping you to formulate a plan of action to help you better cope with depression.

Web Resources for Information on Depression

For symptoms of depression, see
http://www.nmha.org or http://www.lorenbennett.org.

To screen yourself for depression, see
http://www.depression-screening.org.

To talk about depression and to obtain further information, see
http://www.counselingforloss.com.

For information on depression and therapies, including medications,
see http://www.depression.org.

For information concerning post-traumatic stress disorder, see
http://www.ncptsd.org.

For help in choosing a therapist, see

http://www.psychcentral.com/therapst.htm and
    http://www.adec.org.
To contact the American Psychological Association, visit
    http://www.apa.org.
To contact the American Psychiatric Association, visit
    http://www.psych.org.
For holistic health information, contact the American Holistic Health
    Association at http://www.ahha.org.

8. Dreams: One Last Visit

For information about dreams and dream interpretation, see:

Crisp, Tony. *Dream Dictionary: An A to Z Guide to Understanding Your
    Unconscious Mind.* New York: Dell Publishing, 2002.

Jung, Carl. *The Archetypes and the Collective Unconscious.* Vol. 9, pt. 1 of
    Collected Works of C. G. Jung. Princeton, N.J: Princeton University
    Press, 1981.

Mantoon, Mary Ann. *Understanding Dreams.* Woodstock, Conn.: Spring
    Publications, 1984.

Sanford, John. *Dreams and Healing.* New York: Paulist Press, 1979. This
    book provides a more pastoral approach to dreams. Well worth the
    read.

Schoenewolf, Gerald. *A Dictionary of Dream Interpretation.* Northvale,
    N.J.: Jason Aronson Publishers, 1997.

For further information on grief dreams and for general grief support,
    see http://www.griefdreams.com.

9. Faith, Religion, and Spirituality: Where's God in All of This?

For help with prayer, see:

Aycock, Don. M. *Prayer 101: What It Is, What It Isn't, How to Do It.*
    Nashville, TN: Broadman and Holman Publishers, 1998.

Mosley, Glenn, and Joanna Hill. *The Power of Prayer Around the World.*
    Radnor, Pa.: Templeton Foundation Press, 2000.

Postema, Don. *Space for God: The Study and Practice of Prayer and Spiritu-
    ality.* Grand Rapids, Mich.: CRC Publications, 1997.

See also Lewis, C. S. *A Grief Observed.* New York: Bantam Books, 1983.

For sibling support, see http://www.adultsiblinggrief.com.

10. ACCEPTANCE: A SEARCH FOR MEANING

For help in meaning making, see:

Attig, Thomas. *How We Grieve: Relearning the World.* New York: Oxford University Press, 1996.

Breathnach, Sarah Ban. *Simple Abundance.* New York: Warner Books, 1998.

———. *The Simple Abundance Journal of Gratitude.* New York: Warner Books, 1996.

Frankl, Viktor. *Man's Search for Meaning.* New York: Washington Square Press, 1998.

Slan, Joanna Campbell. *Scrapbook Storytelling: Save Family Stories and Memories with Photos, Journaling, and Your Own Creativity.* St. Louis: EFG, 1999.

Smedley, Wendy. *The Complete Idiot's Guide to Scrapbooks.* Indianapolis, Ind.: Alpha Books, 2000.

For online scrapbook help, see: http://www.scrapbook-tips.com.

To create a video memorial, see: http://www.createavideo.com.

Web Resources

Grief (general)

Center for Grief Recovery/Institute for Creativity. Creative grief recovery. Nonprofit organization that offers services for those who are seeking help as well as for professionals. Contact http://www.griefcounselor.bigstep.com.

Crises, Grief & Healing. Specializing in healing from loss. Visit http://www.webhealing.com.

Doors of Hope. Provides support, healing, and help for victims of abuse, bullying, violence, and sudden death. See http://www.doorsofhope.com.

Grief Loss & Recovery. Offers emotional support and friendship. Provides a safe place for the bereaved to share feelings. Contact http://www.grieflossrecovery.com.

Grief Net-Rivendell Resources. Variety of resources related to death, dying, bereavement, and major emotional and physical losses. Visit http://rivendell.org.

Growth House. Site for the bereaved and those who care for them. See http://www.growthhouse.org.

GROWW. Offers a wide range of grief and bereavement resources. Contact http://www.groww.com.

Hope for Bereaved. Provides hope, support, and services for the bereaved. See http://www.hopeforbereaved.com.

Hospice Foundation of America. Death, dying, and bereavement services. Visit http://www.hospicefoundation.org.

GRIEF (SIBLING)

Adult Sibling Grief. A website dedicated to surviving adult siblings. Message board, chat, and memorials.
Visit http://www.adultsiblinggrief.com.

The Compassionate Friends. The largest grief organization in America provides adult sibling grief information.
See http://www.thecompassionatefriends.com.

Julie's Place. A Web Site for Bereaved Siblings: For children and teenagers grieving the loss of a sibling. Message boards, activities, and related information. Contact http://www.Julies place.com.

The Sibling Connection. Huge site with all sorts of activities and information. Contact http://www.siblingconnection.com.

Twinless Twins. Support group for twins (all multiple births) who suffer from the loss of companionship of their twin through death, estrangement, or in utero loss. Visit http://www.twinlesstwins.org.

GRIEF (OTHER)

AirCraft Casualty Emotional Support Services (ACCESS). Peer grief support and information to those who lost loved ones in air disasters. Contact http://www.accesshelp.org.

HALOS (Helping All Loved Ones Survive). Support resource for family and friends who have lost a loved one to homicide.
Visit http://www.halos.org.

HIV/AIDS. See http://www.healingforest.com/bookaids.htm.

The Tragedy Assistance Program for Survivors (TAPS). For those who have lost a loved one who was serving in the armed forces. Visit http://www.taps.org/movie.htm.

Traumatic Death. Site for support of survivors of sudden and traumatic deaths. Contact http://www.journey of hearts. org/jofh/grief/accident.2.

Other Resources

American Association of Suicidology
2459 South Ash Street
Denver, CO 80222
(303) 692-0985
http://www.suicidology.org

Association for Death Education and Counseling
638 Prospect Ave.
Hartford, CT 06105-4298
(203) 232-4825
http://www.adec.org

The Compassionate Friends
P.O. Box 3696
Oak Brook, IL 60522-3696
(877) 969-0010
http://www.compassionatefriends.org

National Organization for Victim Assistance (NOVA)
1730 Park Rd. NW
Washington, DC 20010
(202) 232-8560 / 24-hour Hot Line (202) 393-6683
http://www.try-nova.org

Recommended Reading

Attig, Thomas. *How We Grieve: Relearning the World.* New York: Oxford University Press, 1996.

Aycock, Don. M. *Prayer 101: What It Is, What It Isn't, How to Do It.* Nashville, Tenn.: Broadman and Holman Publishers, 1998.

Bowlby, John. *Attachment and Loss.* Vols. 1–2. New York: Basic Books, 1969–1973. Vol. 3. London: Hogarth Press, 1980.

Breathnach, Sarah Ban. *Simple Abundance: A Daybook of Comfort and Joy.* New York: Warner Books, 1998.

Crisp, Tony. *Dream Dictionary: An A to Z Guide to Understanding Your Unconscious Mind.* New York: Dell Publishing, 2002.

Frankl, Viktor. *Man's Search for Meaning.* New York: Washington Square Press, 1998.

Jung, Carl. *The Archetypes and the Collective Unconscious.* Vol. 9, pt. 1 of *Collected Works of C. G. Jung.* Princeton, N.J.: Princeton University Press, 1981.

Kübler-Ross, Elisabeth. *On Death and Dying.* New York: Macmillan, 1969.

Kushner, Harold S. *When Bad Things Happen to Good People.* New York: Avon, 1997.

Lewis, C. S. *A Grief Observed.* New York: Bantam Books, 1983.

Mantoon, Mary Ann. *Understanding Dreams.* Woodstock, Conn.: Spring Publications, 1984.

Mosley, Glenn, and Joanna Hill. *The Power of Prayer Around the World.* Radnor, Pa.: Templeton Foundation Press, 2000.

Postema, Don. *Space for God: The Study and Practice of Prayer and Spirituality.* Grand Rapids, Mich: CRC Publications, 1997.

Sanford, John. *Dreams and Healing.* New York: Paulist Press, 1979.

Schoenewolf, Gerald. *A Dictionary of Dream Interpretation*. Northvale, N. J.: Jason Aronson Publishers, 1997.

Solomon, Andrew. *The Noonday Demon: An Atlas of Depression*. New York: Scribner, 2001.

Steinpach, Richard. *Why We Live After Death*. Gambier, Ohio: Grail Foundation Press, 1979.

Wolfelt, Alan D. *Death and Grief: A Guide for Clergy and Others Involved in Care of the Bereaved*. Muncie, Ind.: Accelerated Development, 1988.

Wright, Jesse H., and Monica Ramirez Basco. *Getting Your Life Back: The Complete Guide to Recovery from Depression*. New York: Free Press, 2001.

ABOUT THE AUTHOR

T. J. WRAY is an adult sibling survivor who lives in Rhode Island with her husband, three children, and two dogs. She teaches religious studies at Salve Regina University in Newport, Rhode Island, and is the creator of www.adultsiblinggrief.com.